AMONG THE HINDUS

A STUDY OF HINDU FESTIVALS

AMONG THE HINDUS

A STUDY OF HINDU FESTIVALS

R. MANOHAR LALL

GYAN

Published by

Gyan Publishing House
5, Ansari Road
Daryaganj, New Delhi-110002
Phone: 011-47034999, 9811692060
E-mail: books@gyanbooks.com

Distribution Network
gyanbooks.com
India, USA, Canada, UK, Australia, France

ISBN : 978-81-212-3111-4 (PB)
First Published, Cawnpore

2nd Impression 2020

Printed at: Gyan Press, Delhi.

Among the Hindus
Author: R. Manohar Lall

CONTENTS

HINDU MONTHS

The Hindu year—Samvat Era—ordinarily begins in March. It has twelve months except every third year, when it has thirteen months, and this extra month is called Laund. In order to give the reader a general idea of the Hindu months as corresponding to those used in the Christian calendar the different tables are printed below side by side for comparison.

15th March to 15th April	... Chaitra or Chet.
15th April to 15th May	... Vaisakha or Baisakh.
15th May to 15th June	... Jyeshtha or Jeth.
15th June to 15th July	... Ashadha or Asar.
15th July to 15th August	... Shravana or Savan.
15th August to 15th September	... Bhadrapada or Bhadon.
15th September to 15th October	... Ashwin or Asoj.
15th October to 15th November	... Kartikka or Katik.
15th November to 15th December	... Margashirsh or Mangsar.
15th December to 15th January	... Pausha or Poh.
15th January to 15th February	... Magha or Magh.
15th February to 15th March	... Phalgun or Phagun.

LIST OF HINDU FESTIVALS

The following list of Hindu festivals is compiled from a Maharashtra Panchanga—calendar—giving tha names of festivals observed by the Hindus in the Central Provinces.

Chaitra: 1st.—Dhivijaropan, the erecting of the flag. New year day.

9th.—Ramnaumi—the birthday of Ram.

15th.—Hanuman Jayanti—the birthday of Hanuman, the monkey-god.

Vaisakha: 3rd.—Akshya Tritya—Unperishing third.

Jyeshtha: 12th.—Vat Savitri.

Ashadha: 15th.—Vyas Puja.

30th.—Deep Puja. This is a great festival of goldsmiths and silversmiths. They worship their implements and tools this day and pass the day in festivities.

Shravana: 5th.—Nag Panchmi—the fifth, sacred to the snakes.

15th.—Rakshabandhan, tying of threads on the wrist.

Narali Purnima—as observed on the West Coast.

23rd.—Badya Ashtami, Janam Ashtami or Krishna Jayanti, the birthday of the God Krishna.

30th.—Pola, or the cattle festival.

Bhadarpada: 4th.—Ganesh Chathurthi.

8th.—Durga Vahanam or Gauria Vahanam, that is, the establishing or placing of the goddess Durga or Gauri.

9th.—Gauri Pujan, the worshipping of the goddess Gauri.

10th.—Gauri Visarjanam or the immersion of the image of Gauri.

24th.—Avidhva Naumi; this is the day set aside for the performing of certain ceremonies by the husband for the soul of the dead wife. The ceremonies are the same as in the Pitri Moksh, the ceremony performed by the son for the salvation of his dead father.

30th.—Sarva Pitri Moksh Amavasya. This is the day reserved for performing the ceremonies for the dead father and mother.

Ashwin: 10th.—Vijaya Dashmi — the tenth as Victory Day, or Daserah (celebrating Ram's victory over Ravan).

15th.—Koja giri—First fruit, full moon—worship of the goddess Parbati, wife of Shiva.

29th.—Narak Chaturdashi.

30th.—Laxmi Pujan—the worship of the goddess of wealth.

Kartika: 1st.—Bali Pratipada.

Gokridanam, the worship of the cow.

New year of Samvat Era.

2nd.—Yama Dvitiya.

Bhaubij.

Chandar darshan—looking at the new moon—an auspicious thing to do.

12th.—Tulsi Vivaha—the Tulsi plant wedding.

14th.—Vaikanth Chaturdashi.

15th.—Tripuri.

Margashirsh: 6th.—Champa Sheshti.

15th.—Datta Jayanti.

Pausha: Til Sakrant—It has no fixed date.

Magha: 5th.—Basant Panchmi.

13th.—Of the dark half:—Shivratri.

Phagun: 15th.—Holi.

16th.—Dhuli Vandanam—worshipping of the ashes of Holi.

INTRODUCTION

It is difficult and dangerous to generalise about India. The customs and manners which are observed in one part may be wholly unknown in another section of the country. These differences excite little interest among the peoples, for there is nothing strange in the phenomena. There are about 2378 castes and innumerable sub-castes among the Hindus, illustrating the fact, that in India differences are emphasised and proudly maintained. The author can bear witness to the helplessness of the people who groan under the tyranny of these social and religious rites and customs. To extricate themselves from this blood sucking octopus which sends its tentacles into the innermost recesses of Hindu society, is well-nigh impossible. The women of two families of different castes living side by side compare notes on the very expensive ceremonial observances with tears in their eyes. They dare not swerve from the course laid down by their teachers and leaders; so rigid are the dictates of religion.

Enveloped as he is in an atmosphere of religion, the texture of the Hindu's being is made up of the warp and woof of religious ideas and sanctions. And we may say that even while he is in his mother's womb the Hindu is charged with the spirit of religion. Therefore from the cradle to the grave he is preeminently a philosopher and a devotee. The Maharaja on his gaddi and the poor subject in his cottage take a delight in the discussion of the fundamental problems of life. Even some of the educated Hindus who have lost faith in image worship, rites and ceremonies still preserve the same outlook on life as the others. The Hindu woman in particular perpetuates religion in its original form. And very often it is the influence of the women which is the cause of the men adhering to the traditional worship.

The complete transformation of the Hindu family is only a question of time. Hinduism has not been able to keep pace with a progressive world. In recent years however, the old prejudices are vanishing, making the transition from the old to the new easy under the influence of the West. The impact of Christianity on India has also been very effective in introducing certain new ideas and purifying several of the old methods. Perhaps the most noticeable change is the new attitude to life—an attitude which is produced by the adoption of the principles of Jesus Christ.

Invaders have come and gone leaving the Hindu after a little disturbance to settle down to his own quiet and even life, the reason being that the Hindu philosophy of life has proved a bulwark to the religion. Latterly even the self-satisfied Hindu has been drawn into the whirlpool of the new life that is surging within and without him. That section of the people who have hitherto been called the "untouchables" have in recent years asserted their position and have attained a very important status in life. No longer are the restraints of the past binding on them. In South India, the stronghold of the caste system, they are demanding to walk on the same streets as the higher castes and the days are coming when it will be a thing of the past for blacksmiths, carpenters and leather workers to pollute a Brahmin at 24 feet, toddy drawers at 30 feet, Charuman cultivators at 48 feet and Pariah and beef eaters at 64 feet. On the other hand there are a number of schools meant for untouchables only where the highest class of Brahmins teach them and eat things from their hands. There is no doubt that the motive is economic in a large number of cases.

If one were to observe carefully the different festivals, customs and manners of the Hindus one could notice a strange and inexplicable mixture of things—new and old. The progressive is entwined with the conservative and the beautiful with the ugly. The gross is wrapped up with the sublime and the things that are of good report are inextricably mingled with the features of ill report. The result is one of bewilderment and not clearness.

The gods are many and their characteristics are varied. As amongst men and women, even within the hierarchy there is jealousy. Sometimes the gods are jealous of human beings lest the latter should excel them in meritorious doings. Some of the gods are mischievous and full of revenge. They are subject to all the earthly passions—lust, hatred and envy. They are playful, and full of pranks. Some of the gods love solitude while others delight in company. Sometimes they love to be surrounded by courtiers and even by dancing girls. To go about in disguise is not unknown amongst the gods. For they revel in misleading human beings. The goddesses have not infrequently shown their ability to dominate and direct the courses of their husbands. These gods hold sway each over his own domain. And some are a kind of absentee landlords. These gods which are many and endowed with diverse gifts number about 330 million.

Brahma is the Creator Vishnu the Preserver and Protector and Shiva the Destroyer—this last being the most dreaded of all. Shiva is considered the head of the triad. Brahma has hardly any temple to his name due to his uttering a falsehood when he was sent out to find out the top end of Shiva's linga. Brahma did not continue his search to the end but tried to mislead Shiva. Shiva laid a curse on him. Hence the absence of temples in honour of Brahma. Brahma is said to have been born from the lotus navel of Vishnu, and is said to be the advocate of the gods in heaven, where he represents their case to Vishnu. He fell in love with his daughter Satarupa. Once when she made a circumambulation around her father, he had an intense desire to follow her movement but on account of delicacy of feelings he did not think it proper to do so, but lo, five faces immediately appeared on his neck facing in four directions and on top, and was thus able to have the pleasure of watching the bewitching movements of his daughter whom he later on married, and thus created a son Manu, the Adam of the world.

Brahma lost his fifth face as a result of a fight with Mahesvara in the body of Kalabhairva. In a dispute between Vishnu and Brahma as to who was the lord of the universe, one Katurveda rejected the claims of the both and decided in favour of Mahesvara, thus antagonising both of them. When Brahma gave a look of wrath from his top face, it was decapitated by Mahesvara in the fierce fight that ensued. He now has four faces and four arms and rides on a chariot drawn by seven swans.

In India, only two of the three chief gods are worshipped. Hindus are therefore divided into the two main groups—Vaishnavas and Saivites. Vaishnavites consider Vishnu all-important while the

Saivites hold Shiva in great esteem. These attachments lead to persistent quarrels between the illiterate and orthodox followers of the two gods, constant argument and verbal combat characterising all these conflicts. They ridicule each other's observances by offering sometimes, dirty interpretations. Yet there are days which are observed by both the sects in common. In the central parts of the country there is not much antagonism between the two. They observe each other's days with almost equal respect to both.

Vishnu has ten incarnations — Ramchandar, Krishna, Rama-with-the axe, Vaman-Dwarf, Fish, Tortoise, Boar, Man-lion, Budha—(it is said that Vishnu appeared in this incarnation in order to beguile the world into the wrong faith). Kalki autar has not yet appeared. He will come during the millenium. Kala Bhairva is considered a manifestation of Shiva. He has a big temple in Benares. As he was black and was always followed by a black dog, so in the streets a black dog is held in peculiar veneration. He is generally well fed by the people in order perhaps to please Shiva. Quite a number of people desire to die within the holy precincts of the Kala Bhairva temple in Benares so that they may be saved from being born again in this world. The author once saw in the Central Provinces Kala Bhairva being worshipped by means of five stones, one placed in front of four other stones arranged in a line and a black dog fed on excellent food. Shiva has no incarnations except Kala Bhairva. But he is worshipped in other forms. But Shiva and Vishnu have incarnations of their combined Sakti—Energy.

Besides these incarnations there are scores of objects which are worshipped and held in veneration. People worshipped nature in its many aspects —trees and plants, animals, the sun, the moon, the planets and the stars, and finally the seasons. They observe auspicious and inauspicious days and times. They believe also in the existence of ghosts and spirits who are propitiated lest they harm human beings. There are goddesses whose help is invoked for minor purposes. Some diseases are traced to certain other goddesses. They are called Matas—mothers. Our earth is also called "Mother" because she sustains us. Mother earth is supposed to be subject to all the physical changes that human existence is heir to. She is supposed to have her regular periods. These days are observed by the Hindus. The rainy season is utilised to fulfil mother earth's desire for cleanliness. The season of ploughing and sowing is akin to her conceiving and in due course she delivers her ripened crops till her next period of uncleanliness arrives.

Every epidemic is considered to have some presiding Mata. For instance, the goddess of small Pox is called 'Sitla'. When people suffer from this disease, the Mata is supposed to have appeared in that particular individual's house. The women then go in a procession to a temple, or to some idol by the way-side, to sacrifice a goat with the usual accompaniments of vermillion, rice, incense. In epidemics like Cholera and Plague, the people get together in a central place, and then proceed to march with an effigy of the disease. The words Ram Ram Sat Hai "God alone is true" are used in the chants. And finally the effigy is carried outside the village, the idea being that the goddess of that particular disease has been driven outside the village limits. The common understanding is that the vanished Mata appears in the adjoining village. By this process, after being driven from village to village, the disease is said to disappear either into a distant country or into the sea. No kind of injury should be inflicted on the Mata. No effort should be made to stamp the disease out of a village. This is the reason why some of these epidemics spread so rapidly in India, without disappearing altogether!

In India almost everything is considered to have life. Anything that is useful is held in awe and veneration. The author's cook had to withdraw from one place to cook in another house at short notice. But the cook delayed going, and was busy cleaning the fireplace. On enquiry, the cook replied that he would be considered lacking in gratitude to the spirit if he left the place unswept. It is believed in some parts of India that if you spit in fire, your mouth will be full of sores. If you drop a piece of bread on the ground you must pick it up and kiss it immediately. If you do not want to eat it, you may give the morsel to a bird or an animal. To sit on books, or in any other manner to show disrespect to them, is considered equivalent to insulting Saraswati, the goddess of learning. Instances could be multiplied to prove that any agency of usefulness should, in the thought of the people of India, be treated with considerable respect.

As has been mentioned above, the gods have their own domains. Their work is divided each minding his own business. But they are sometimes afraid of demons and of men also. When they are unable to overcome their enemies they go in deputation to the chief gods whose assistance helps them to maintain their dignity. They sometimes behave like weak human beings.

The manner of the birth of the gods is not after the way of men. There is nothing extraordinary about them. Sita, the wife of an incarnation of Vishnu was born of a furrow. Karna was born out of the ear of Kunti; children have been born by the mere looks of a pious but lustful sage. The cut up bits of a child born through miscarriage have grown up into full size babies. The wife of Shiva made the god Ganesh with the dirt of her skin while bathing. Shiva, Vishnu and Brahma created a woman by means of their combined thick and mist-like breath.

Certain of the gods have a weakness for beautiful women. Some gods are faithful to their wives. There are goddesses living in the heavens and if the gods so decree, the beautiful women of this earth can be transformed into goddesses. Some gods are very passionate and lustful. A god's attention can be drawn by beautiful but naked women of this earth. If a god is busy elsewhere his attention can be attracted easily if urgently required. Ordinarily gods have got to be reminded about certain things. Curiously enough they are not omnipresent and omniscient. In the temples the gongs are struck and bells are rung not only to rouse them from their deep sleep but also to inform them, in the same manner, of their dinner and breakfast. There is no Hindu temple in India where the bells are not rung and the gongs are not struck.

As a six-years old boy the author had occasion to witness the extraordinary ceremony of attracting the attention of Indra, the thunderer, the rain god, the god of Swarga or paradise. A dozen young women, two of them being nearer middle age, the fair and handsome looking wives and daughters of farmers, whose dependence on rains is well-known, came together in a courtyard and commenced dancing naked under the canopy of the threatening clouds.

Each woman sang and danced for fifteen seconds praying to God for rain. The ceremony was followed by heavy rain. It should not be inferred that the women were lacking in the sense of modesty because though they had to remove their clothes quite early till the actual time for dancing arrived, they were hiding their shame with the clothes in their laps. When her turn came each woman setting aside her clothes danced in a circle turning first to the right and then to the left. The impression left on the author's mind was that those who participated in the ceremony did so with a certain amount of merriment. There was no seriousness. Though the women were shy they laughed among themselves. This strange performance of nude women created a weird feeling in the mind of the author. For it reminded him of the story of the witches dancing in a darkened atmosphere to the accompaniment of clouds. The object of the dance was to attract the attention of the god who might be busy with other affairs.

A god is not known to lead a lonely life. Both in the heavens and on earth gods have their courtiers and wives about them in their durbars. The presence of devadasis is explained away by the excuse that it is providing company for the gods. The women dance before the gods within the temple and while they are in procession. The Brahmins who are supposed to represent the god very often abuse the privilege and gross immorality prevails in certain places.

It is said that the stories of the gods and their doings should not be taken literally. There is a spiritual interpretation revealing a deep mystical meaning. The amatory tendencies of the gods should not be associated with base inclinations. The contention is that the gods in some of these deeds come down to the level of even the lowest of mankind thereby making it possible for the least initiated to understand the ways of the Divine.

A correspondent writing to 'The Epiphany' of Calcutta about Sri Krishna says: "Sri Krishna, the Herald King of Mathura—nurtured in the abode of the bucolic chief of Gokul—is the eighth incarnation of Vishnu, one of the deities of the Hindu triad. He is the embodiment of all that attracts the human heart, love, music and beauty.

"The "Lilas" (sports and diversions) of the Divine Cow-herd are but the similitudes to the eternal varieties of the highest religion. Playing upon the flute on the banks of the Jumna He pours forth His sweetened melodious strains and the river swells up in an ecstasy, trying to touch the lotus-like feet of our lord Krishna. Similarly the heart of a seeker-after-him leaps up with joy like the surges of the Jamuna when he listens to the melliferous call of His ambrosial voice.

"The "Gopis" or the village maidens of Brindaban repair to the river Jamuna in order to perform their ablution. They take off their clothes from their persons and keeping them on the bank enter the river to sport themselves merrily in the water. Stealthily taking away their garments Sri Krishna climbs up a "Kadamba" tree (Nauclea Cadamba) situated on the bank. He refuses to restore the apparels to the damsels, unless they come out of the water and beg for them with the palms of their folded hands. The deeper significance underlying the allegory is that Sri Krishna stands for the Over-Soul or the Supreme Spirit, whereas the virgins collectively represent the sentient human soul which must know itself in its most hideous nakedness before it can ask for the grace of the Over-Soul.

"The "Rasa-Lila" (or the amorous sports held between Krishna and the milkmaids of Brindaban) poetically illustrates the orderly dance of the Cosmic forces. Each force manifests itself in pairs—male and female. The whole cosmos dances with the music of Sri Krishna by the rhythmic movements of the twin-forces.

"The vision of Sri Krishna has been India's vision throughout the ages. Nations as well as individuals perish for want of vision. The Hindu India lost her pristine glory and greatness when she lost the spiritual vision for which Sri Krishna stands"

The Epiphany of Calcutta writing under the heading of "A Last Refuge"* says as follows:—"The last refuge of the defenders of polytheism and its attendant mythology is the attempt to maintain that the stories of the gods are capable of deep mystical and spiritual interpretations which make them alike the vehicle of noble doctrine and the inspiration of a truly religious life. It was when polytheism in the Graeco-Roman world was about to fall, undermined as a system of credible theism by the new moral sense which Christianity was gradually but surely diffusing amongst mankind, that educated men, and indeed accomplished writers such as Plutarch, attempted to prop it up by pretending that by allegorizing these unpleasant and immoral stories deep spiritual truths could be conveyed to man.

"It would be well if Hindus would remember that there is nothing really distinctive in their polytheism. Point by point it is exactly the same in its expression in worship and practice as was that old polytheism which long ago was abolished in Europe and North Africa. Hinduism is simply another name for the old Graeco-Roman religion; India is the one land of the whole world in which this exploded polytheism still survives. Plutarch, as we have said, attempted the method of allegorization, but it was the last refuge of a discredited cult. It was easily demolished by the application of a little commonsense, and men

* Reproduced by the kind permission of the Editor—

came to see that a system which violated reason and outraged moral decency could not be defended by attaching to its myths and stories meanings with which they had not in reality the remotest connection. It was obvious that children taught these stories and given these explanations straightway proceeded to remember the indecencies and to forget their so-called "spiritual" interpretation. At the philosophical congress held a short time ago in Calcutta Rabindranath Tagore in his presidential address referred to the advice which Plato gave as to the expulsion of poets from the ideal republic, but he did not (in the report we read) explain why Plato had given this advice. It was because the poets so largely occupied themselves with the stories of the gods and goddesses and their highly improper behaviour that, for the sake of the children who would naturally think that being gods and goddesses their conduct might rightly be imitated, it were expedient for the State to banish them altogether. Plato was a far greater man than Plutarch and did not shrink from facing facts. You cannot prop up an immoral system of mythology by tieing to it "mystical" interpretations. Adultery, fornication, drunkenness and lying remain ugly things whether they are attributed to deities or men, and all the "spiritual" explanations in the world will not build up out of such material a religion of true and pure monotheism which may serve as the inspiration of a really holy life.

"But when we arrive at a last defence we may hope that the fall of the citadel of error is near; even the Hinderburg line was pierced at last. The very fact that educated Hindus are beginning to realize that no other defence of the gods and their conduct is even possible points to the ultimate and inevitable fall of the system. The immensity of the population of India, the lack of education amongst the vast majority, the leaving of the women even of the well-to-do classes mostly untaught, are the causes of the prolonged survival of polytheism and idolatry in this land, although it has perished almost everywhere else. It has also obtained an added lease of existence (we will not say "life") owing to the mistaken idea that Hinduism and nationalism are bound together in one bundle, and that a true patriot must not desert the shrines of the gods. Kali and country are felt somehow to belong to one another, and because the Krishna-Radha cult had its origin in India therefore true sons of India must uphold it at all costs. But again this cannot last. Men's vision is bound to get clearer, and truths will come out in their true perspective. If India is ever to be one it will be because the principle of spiritual liberty is universally recognized, and spiritual liberty carries with it the implication that true religion is not only supernatural but it is also supernational. Hinduism ought no more to be bound up with patriotism than Christianity or Buddhism. The Indian must be spiritually free, a loyal, loving citizen of the Kingdom of God without any diminution of his loyal love to his mother land, but rather with an increase of it.

"What is now more necessary than anything is for students calling themselves Hindus to face the facts. They do not read the shastras and only have vaguest ideas of what they contain. When they are confronted with passages which describe the gods as drunken and immoral they simply refer us to some writer who has "spiritualized" these incidents and given us their true meaning.

"If it be urged that it is only in the later Hindu books that these low and degrading descriptions of the gods can be found and that a pure monotheism is to be found in the Vedas, careful and open-minded examination of them will demonstrate that this belief is without foundation. The Brahmans are "that part of the Veda which was intended for the use and guidance of Brahmans in the use of the hymns of the Mantra, but the Brahmans, equally with the Mantra, is held to be Sruti or revealed word". Let us look at the Brahmans with a view to finding the conception of deity which they teach. We shall find that the Aitareya-Brahman (vi. II) charges the gods with drunkenness; prohibition does not prevail among them. "The gods get drunk, as it were, at the midday libation, and are then consequently at the third libation in a state of complete drunkenness". And these words are really a commentary on the Rig-Veda viii. 58. II "Indra has drunk, Agni has drunk, all the gods have become exhilarated". Lovers of wine are frequently depicted as lovers of women, and the gods are also thus represented in the Satapatha-Brahmana vi. 5. In the Shadvinsha Brahmana of the Sama Veda a ceremony is prescribed in which the god Indra is to be invoked in these words; "O adulterous lover of Ahalya".

"In these days when the removal of untouchability is so frequently talked and written about and so little is done to remove it, save by Christian workers, it is sad to notice that the Sataphata-Brahmana teaches that "The gods talk only to the upper castes" (xi. 4. 4. I). The god Indra always acted on the principle that all is fair in love and war, and so we find him not only using a mean trick against his enemies, but also addressed by his own priest at the altar in these unworthy words, "Come, O Indra! Come, O Lord of the bay steeds! Ram of Medhatihi! Wife of Vrishanasva! Best riding buffalo! Lover of Ahalya! Thereby, he (*i.e.* the priest performing the ceremony) wishes him joy in these affairs of his".

"It is things like these that have to be mystically interpreted, taken not from the later books, but from Sruti. Can any reasonable man maintain that it is a method consonant with the Divine Holiness to enshrine His revelation in images which by themselves draw men to think lightly of drunkenness, deceit, and lust?"

THE KALIYUGA

A Yuga in Sanskrit (in Heb. Olim, in Gr. Aion, and in Lat. Ævum) means an age of the world. Four Yugas are recognised by the Hindu mythology, the Krita, the Treta, the Dvapara and the Kali. All these four Yugas joined together constitute a great age, or an aggregate of four ages (Mahayuga). A thousand such aggregates are a day of Brahma. Let us give the number of years allotted to each Yuga in the years of the gods and in the years of men. The first rule is that a year of men is equal to a day of the gods. The following table gives the years of the four Yugas according to both these calculations:—

Yugas.	Divine years.	Years of Mortals.
Krita	4,800	4,800 × 360 = 1,728,000
Treta	3,600	3,600 × 360 = 1,296,000
Dvapara	2,400	2,400 × 360 = 864,000
Kali	1,200	1,200 × 360 = 432,000
	Total (a Mahayuga)	4,320,000

So the notion of these four ages may be best remembered by a deteriorating series expressed by a descending arithmetical progression as 4, 3, 2, 1, by the conversion of units into thousands and by the legend that these are divine years each composed of 360 years of men. A period of 4,320,000 years constitutes a great age, or a Mahayuga, and this number multiplied by 1,000 *i.e.*, 4,320,000,000 years becomes a day of Brahma :—

Daivikanam Yuganam tu sahasram parisamkhyaya
Brahmam-ekamaharjneyam tavati ratrir eva cha.

At the end of this day a dissolution of the universe will occur, when all the three worlds, earth and the regions of space will all be consumed by fire. The three worlds then become but one mighty ocean. Brahma will sleep for a night, of equal duration with his day, on this ocean and at its close will create the world anew. A year of Brahma is composed of 360 such days and nights and a hundred such years constitute his whole life, which is called a Kalpa.

The word "Kaliyuga" is constantly cropping up in Indian writings and speeches, and is likely to do so still more in the future, but a perusal of this article will explain the belief, for a superstition it cannot fairly be called, based as it is on writings held sacred by the people. That extraordinary divine, Dr. Cumming, used to startle periodically worthy British matrons and susceptible young men and maidens by proving to his and their complete satisfaction that the end of the world was near at hand. His prophecies were the result of abstruse mathematical calculations based on his interpretation of certain scriptural texts;......... .... The point, however, on which particular stress is to be laid is the difficulty that must naturally exist in dealing with people who honestly believe in this Kaliyuga story during such a crisis as the present. Even the most sceptical will read with some surprise of the evils accompanying the close of this age, as described in the Vishnu Purana. They tally so closely with recent changes in the social order of Hindu life.—Editor, The Madras Mail

Brahma-naschayusha Kalpa kalpavidbhih nirupitah.

Such, in brief is the belief of the Hindus regarding the ages and the duration of the world and full details of this belief will be found in Books I, IV, V and VI of the Vishnu Purana.

What is the object of Brahma in thus destroying the whole universe and recreating it ? The Hindu philosophy most beautifully explains it :—

Sarva-bhutani Kaunteya
Prakritam yanti mamikam,
Kalpa-kshaye punas-tani
Kalpadau visrijamy-aham.

"I absorb the whole universe in myself at the end of the Kalpa and at its commencement I create it again," says Brahma. Volumes are written in the several Puranas about the merits and demerits of each Yuga, or age. The brief way to remember the whole subject would be to imagine Virtue to have four legs. In the Krita, or the first Yuga, Virtue walks on all her four legs. In the Treta, or the second Yuga, she walks only on three of her legs; in the Dvapara on two, and in the last age, the Kaliyuga, on only one leg. After this brief remark about the Hindu notions of the age of the universe, its destruction and recreation, let us confine ourselves on the present occasion to the full description of the Kaliyuga, the fourth Hindu age which is current now, and in which Virtue is said to walk only on one of her four legs. The Kaliyuga era commenced in 3102 B. C.

and we are now in the year 4998 of the Kaliyuga; *i.e.*, 4,997 years of the Kaliyuga have already passed away and the year current 4998 commenced on the 12th April, 1896. The year 5000 of the Kaliyuga will commence on the 12th April, 1899, A. D. and end on the 11th April 1900*. The belief of the orthodox Hindus from the Himalayas to Cape Comorin that this, their fourth, era is one of vice, wickedness and misery is universal, and is recorded in almost each and every one of their Puranas. It is also strongly believed that the year 5000 of the Kaliyuga will be a year of doom and ruin. Let us dwell at length on both these beliefs.

In Book IV of the Vishnu Purana it is stated that Kali feared to set his feet on this world as long as it was purified by the touch of the sacred feet of Krishna.

Yavat sapada padamabhyam
Sprisan-aste Ramapatih,
Tavat Kalir vai prithivim
Parakrantum na ch-asakat.

The usual notion of the Hindus is that the age of Kali set in from the death of Krishna; but it is also a common supposition that it commenced a little later, with the reign of Parikshit. It is said in Book II of the Bhagavata that after Krishna died or ascended to his abode in Heaven, the Pandavas also followed him after installing their grandson and heir, Parikshit, as

*5032 years of Kaliyuga passed away on the 11th April, 1932.

the Emperor of the Bharata. The new monarch, according to the usual custom, set out on a tour round his empire to establish order, to make friends with friendly kings and to subdue vassals. He finished his tour and was returning to his capital, when, on his way back and near the river Sarasvati he noticed that a cow and an ox were being tortured to death by a person who appeared to be a Sudra, and who had put on royal robes. The cruel Sudra had cut off three of the four legs of the ox and was proceeding to cut off the fourth leg also. The cow appeared to be only a bag of bones; she was so lean and dried up by starvation. Even a heart of adamant would have melted away at the sight. But the Sudra went on kicking and lashing her incessantly. Parikshit was horrified at what he saw and in great wrath addressed the person as follows:— "Who are you, vile wretch, that have put on royal garments? Are you not ashamed of your conduct towards these poor creatures, one of which you have already deprived of its three legs and the other you have starved to death? I must put you at once to death." The Emperor then asked the ox and the cow to relate their history. After some reluctance the ox said that he was Justice (or Virtue, Dharama) who walked on his four legs of (1) contemplation upon God, (2) purity of life, (3) mercy towards living beings, and (4) truth in the Krita yuga or first Hindu age; that he had lost his three legs at the rate of one at the end of every

Yuga and that he had his only leg, truth, left remaining at the commencement of the Kali era and that lord of the Kaliyuga was already aiming at his fourth leg. The Emperor learnt the cow to be the goddess Earth who was reduced to that condition by the departure of Krishna, from this world of men. Parikshit was horrified at what he saw and heard, and aimed his death-dealing sword at the Sudra, when, wonder of wonders ! he threw away his royal garments, assumed his true form and falling down before the Emperor, begged for his life. This Sudra was Kali himself. Parikshit was a true hero and a genuine sprout of the Pandava family. His motto was, never kill a fallen enemy. So he spared Kali's life on condition that he left his dominions at once. But Kali begged for some place to live in. He was asked by the Emperor to find his abode in gambling houses, in taverns, in women of unchaste lives, in slaughtering places and in gold. And Kali agreed to do so. So, as long as Parikshit reigned over the Bharata (India) Kali confined himself only to these five places; but after the reign of that just Emperor, Kali made his way to other places like wild fire and established his power throughout the length and breadth of the whole world. This, in short is the legend of the setting in of the Kaliyuga.

In India, when a young boy or girl happens to break, in eating or dress, the othodox rules of caste, his or her parents will say: "O ! It is all the result of the Kaliyuga." If a Hindu becomes a convert to any other religion, or if any atrocious act is committed the Hindu will observe: "O! It is the ripening of Kali." Every deviation from the established custom, every vice, every crime, in fact everything wicked, is set down by the ordinary Hindu to the ascending power of the Lord of the Kali age. These notions entertained by the people must not be entirely set down to be wholly superstitious. In every one of the Hindu Puranas the Kaliyuga (or the dark age) is described as the worst period of everything wrong, unhappy or miserable. The Vishnu Purana, Bhagavata, Devibhagavata, and a number of religious works give a glowing description of the numerous miseries reserved for mankind in the Kaliyuga, and the ordinary Hindu bred up from his infancy in the Puranic lore has accepted these beliefs as part and parcel of his existence, and anything going wrong in his own household or round about him is set down to the influence of the Kali age. Parasara describes the evils of Kaliyuga in detail in the Vishnu Purana. We will give some of the most prominent ones here:—The strict rules of caste, order and observances will never exist. The rights enjoined by the four Vedas will perish. The rules of conduct between the husband and wife, between the preceptor and his disciple will be disregarded. Marriage rules will be set at naught. Every book will be a sacred book. All gods will be gods. People will turn proud at small possessions. Wives will desert their husbands when the latter become poor and take up persons who are rich. A person possessing money will be the lord of everything, irrespective of his birth or position in life. All money will be spent on mere show. The world will become avaricious. Men will desire to acquire wealth by dishonest means. Cows will be fed only as long as they supply milk. The people will ever remain in fear of famine and scarcity. They will ever be watching the sky for a drop of rain. Severe famines will rage and people will be driven to the necessity of living upon leaves of trees. There will never be abundance or pleasure in the Kali age. Kings, instead of protecting their subjects, will plunder them under the pretence of levying taxes. Men of all degrees will believe themselves to be equal to Brahmans. Everyone who happens to have cars, elephants or steeds will fancy himself to be a Rajah. There will be no warriors or Princes who could be called by such names on account of their birth. People will desert their houses. Children will die in great numbers. Women will bear children at the age of 5, 6 or 7 and men beget them when they are 8, 9 or 10. Grey hair will appear when a person is only 12 years of age and the duration of life for men will only be 20 years. The Vedas, the gods, the Brahmans, the sacred waters, will all be disregarded. The parents-in-law will be respected in the place of parents and brothers-in-law (brothers of wives) will be one's bosom friends. Sins will be committed daily and everything which brings down misery on human beings will be found to be prevailing to the greatest extent in the Kali age.

This is but a part of the description given in one of the greatest of the Hindu Puranas on the evils of the Kali age. The railway carriage where a Brahman and a non-Brahman sit side by side in the same compartment and the schools where English is taught in the same way to a Brahman as to a non-Brahman, instead of exciting the admiration of the orthodox Hindu for the benefits they have conferred upon the public, are looked upon as the platforms where Kali plays most for levelling caste distinctions. Female education, though authorities exist in the Puranas themselves for such a course, is viewed as another turn which Kali has taken to corrupt womankind. The several Government and Municipal taxes are considered to be the miseries of the mighty reign of Kali without the least consideration that the subject is bound to pay to the State for his own protection. The Hindu mind is ever ingenious in looking upon everything from a Kali point of view. But we must, at the same time, mention here that it is only the Hindu who lives in remote villages and who has not had the advantage of a free education who thinks thus. Every educated Hindu, of course, takes the right view of the case. Thus ends our description of the Kaliyuga in general and of the evils thereof as found in the Puranas and as prevailing among the people.

In addition to this belief there is yet another, and a strong one, that the year 5000 of the Kaliyuga (April 1899 — April 1900) will be a year of doom and ruin. The famine that is threatening now a great portion of India, the grain riots everywhere, the failure of monsoons, the bubonic plague in Bombay, the several fires and floods in almost all the great rivers (Mahanadis) this year, such as the Krishna, Godavari, Kaveri, Narbada and Tapti, which have caused immense loss of lives and property, are believed by the uneducated classes to be ushering us into a period of general cataclysms which is expected to take place in the last days of 1899 A. D. We will examine now the sources of the belief. Although all the Puranas are unanimous in describing the miseries of the Kali age there is fortunately only one Purana which speaks of the ruin of the world in the year 5000 of the Kali age. But this one Purana is the greatest authority to the whole of India. Its name is the Devibhagvata and it is regarded as a most sacred book. In the 6th chapter of Book IX it is related that the three godesses Sarasvati, Ganga and Lakshmi had a quarrel among themselves in heaven and each cursed the other. By the power of the curses they were converted into the rivers of Sarasvati, Ganga (Ganges) and Padmavati in this world and are expiating their sins here. Lakshmi in addition to her form as the river Padmavati has assumed also the shape of the shrub Tulasi (*Oscymum sanctum*). In the 8th chapter it is stated that these goddesses will abondon this world in the year 5000 of the Kaliyuga and with the disappearance of these noble rivers everything will disappear from the world with the exception of two places — Benares and Brindavan (Muttra). The original in Sanskrit stands thus :—

Kalau pancha sahasram cha
Varsham sthitva cha Bharate,
Jagmus-tas-cha sarit rupam
Vihaya Sri-hareh padam (1)

Yani sarvani tirthani
Kasi Brindavanam vina
Yasyanti sarvam tabhih-cha
Vaikuntham ajnaya Hareh (2)

(1) They—the goddesses Sarasvati, Ganga and Lakshmi, after having stayed in this world for 5,000 years of the Kaliyuga in the shape of rivers, gave up their transformed shapes and went to the abode of Vishnu (heaven).

(2) All other holy things, too, with the exception of Kasi (Benares) and Brindavan (Muttra) accompanied them to the abode of Hari by the order of Hari.

The statement contained in the above two verses is believed to be the highest authority for the impending doom in the year named. Except Benares and Brindavan, everything holy will disappear from the world. The year 5000 of the Kaliyuga occurs in two other places also in the Devibhagavata, once in the middle of Chapter 7 of Book IX when Narayana pronounces the liberation of the curse to the goddesses:—

Kalau pancha sahasre cha
Gate varshe cha mokshanam

'When 5,000 years of the Kali age have expired you will be liberated from the curse'. Again in Chapter 13 (1st verse) where Narada asks Narayana to relate to him what happened to the goddesses after the year 5000, he says:—

Kalau pancha-Sahasrabde
Samatite Suresvara
Kva gata so Mahabhaga
Tanme vyakhyatum arhasi

Thus from a minute examination of the Devibhagavata, the year 5000 is alluded to in only three places in Chapter 8, 9 and 13 of the ninth book of that work. And it is only in Chapter 8 that the disappearance of everything from the world in the year 5000 Kaliyuga is alluded to. And the Hindu belief in the Puranas is that everything happens as predicted therein and even so the doom and ruin of the year 5000 will come to pass as foretold by the Devibhagavata.

In addition to the Puranic belief there are a few verses current among the astrologers of India which imply that the Hindu religion will perish in the year

5000 of the Kali age They are as follows:—

Kalau pancha-sahasrante
Vishnuh tyakshyati medinim (*1*)
Yada Vishnur-divam gachchhet
Tada Veda-viparyasah (*2*)
Yada Veda-viparyasah
Tada jyotir-divam vrajet (*3*)
Tasmat-tu pancha-sahasram
Phala-sastram Kalau yuge (*4*)

They mean (1) Vishnu abandons this world at the close of the year 5000 of the Kaliyuga. (2) When Vishnu goes away, the Vedas will be turned upside down, (3) When the Vedas have suffered thus, the splendour of the planets will vanish. (4) So, the truths of astrology will be current in this world only up to the year 5000 of the Kaliyuga. These verses, which allude to the ruin of India three years hence, are said to have been uttered by Krishnamisra, a poet who flourished in the Court of Vikramaditya at Ujjain in the 11th Century A.D. These are the only sources for the strong Hindu belief that the year 5000 will bring general ruin to the whole world. Some are charitable in stating that if the whole world is not ruined, thore will be wonderful changes and utter misery and famine at least in that year. At what timo of the year 5000 will this ruin overcome India will be the next question.

In the Hindu calendar every month has a zodiac called Rasi with the position of the planets for the month indicated in it by astronomical calculations, Generally not more than a single planet will be found in each of the 12 houses, or mansions, of the Zodiac. Rarely two or three or even four will be found once in several years in one and the same mansion. But if more than four of the planets are found combined in the same house a great calamity is foreseen. The following verses of the Juotisha Sastra may be read with interest:—

Pancha griha hanti samasta desan
Shashta griha hanti samasta bhupan
Sapta grihu hanti samasta lokan
Nirmartyam ashta griha samyutena

They mean that the combination of five planets in one of the mansions of the Zodiac in any month will lead to the destruction of all countries; the combination of six planets, to the destruction of all Kings; that of seven, to the destruction of all worlds, and if eight planets combine the universe will be rendered destitute of men. Bhishma the just and the greatest warrior of the world fell in the wars of the Mahabharata in the month of Magrasira (December) on the new moon day - Amavasa - when seven planets combined in a single mansion of the zodiac of that month. But for that combination such a mighty warrior would never have fallen. This is the belief of the Hindus. The year 1896 A. D., is, as we have stated already, 4998 of the Kaliyuga corresponding to the year Durmukhi of the Brihaspati cycle of 60 years. Five thousand Kaliyuga will be 1899 A. D. and the year Vikari of the Brihaspati cycle. According to the astronomical calculations of the Hindus, eight planets meet in the mansion of Scorpio (Vrichchhika) of the Zodiac of the month of Krittika, corresponding to the last week of November, 1899, at the 23rd Ghatika i. e. 2-6 A. M. on the 13th lunar day (trayodasi) of the dark half of that month. Between that time and the succeeding new moon day, i. e , two days after that combination a great ruin will come over India. India may not be entirely depopulated or devoured by floods, but famine, pestilence, war and other miseries will reign over the whole country. This is the strong belief and November 1899 is the expected time.

What a firm hold this belief has taken possession of the Hindu mind will become plain to our readers if they refer to the Madras Mail of the 24th October last. It will be found there that an astrologer addressed the Dewan in the Mysore Representative Assembly held in October last to make provision for performing pujas (worship) to the planets and to propitiate them to avert the impending catastrophe of the year Vikari, (1899 A. D.), Kaliyuga 5000. Some of the members appeared to have been seriously occupied with that matter. The Dewan promised to place the subject before the Maharajah. Eight planets, it is said, according to the astronomical calculations in this country, meet together in November 1899, in the mansion of Scorpio. and not six as the Mysore astrologer stated. Some astrologers say that the meeting of the eight planets is imposible and that only seven meet in one mansion. A Tamil Pandit and astrologer named Mr. Kandaswami Pillai, of Dindigul, in the Madura District, predicted some time ago that the year 1899 — Kali 5000 — will be one of terrible famine far exceeding that of 1877 in its horrors by reason of the conjunction of the Sun, Mars, Mercury, Venus, Jupiter, Saturn and also the Solar node (Rahu) at one and the same sign of the Zodiac Scorpio in November, 1899.

But let us all be more hopeful. The annals of India show a regular series of famines separated by intervals of not more than 3 to 8 years, some times 10, and lasting frequently over a year, even as long as three years. The most prolonged famine that India ever experienced was that of 1876-78. The S. W. Monsoon failed in 1875 and 1876. The N. E. Monsoon did not bring in sufficient amount of rain in these years. Between 1876-78 people died in thousands. Whatever the uneducated Hindu may say about the horrors of Kali, these famines must be attributed more to the peculiar position of the mountains in India, especially in the Deccan and Southern India. This interferes with the even distribution of rain. We are fortunately at the end of 1896 A. D. Whatever may be the popular belief about the end of the world in November, 1899, let us only suppose that if any calamity at all is ever to happen as predicted by the Puranas, that the years 1897–99 will be a period of prolonged famine as that of 1876–78. Fearing that such may be the case, apart from the puranic ideas, the Government and the charitable public, as would now and then be seen from the columns of the Madras Mail, are already adopting measures to avert its evils.

The year 5000 of Kali is the turning point of a minor cycle of 5000 years commencing from Krishna. It is believed by the Occultists that spirituality gains ascendency after 5000 Kaliyuga. It is quite natural to expect such extraordinary events to take place during the time of the change of either major or minor cycle.

Reproduced from The Madras Mail of 19th Nov: 1896, by the kind permission of the Editor.

TIL SANKRANT

THIS festival has no fixed date, but it generally falls in the month of January ; though in some respects, its significance is equivalent to that of the 21st December, when the season changes and the days begin to lengthen. It is believed that from this date, Day begins in the regions of the gods, and Night in the realms of the *rakshasas* (demons). Since the gods enjoy daylight from this day, we feel happy with them, and celebrate this day as a festival. The word "Sankrant" means crossing. On this day the sun finishes the crossing of 'Dhan Rasi' and begins to cross 'Makar Rasi'. Hence this festival is also called the Makar Sankrant. Again, Sankranti is considered to be a goddess who from this day begins her journey over the world in order to destroy evil in it. Hence this festival is mostly performed by females. They go to one another's houses, interchange new products of the earth, such as til, sugarcane, plums, etc., etc., and ask one another to remain always on friendly terms. This is called Oti Bharan. They say "mitha mitha khao aur mitha mitha bolo". "(Here, take) and eat (these) sweet things and talk sweetly"; (that is, be a sweet-tempered lady). It is commonly believed that the things which she, the goddess, receives become either dear, or are destroyed.

The reason why it is called 'Til Sankrant' is that from this day, days begin to grow longer and increase 'til by til';—'til' being a very minute seed called in English 'sesamum'. People give each other til seeds, plain or mixed with jaggery or made into some sort of preparation. There are scores of ways in which til can be utilized in making different sorts of pastries.

As has been mentioned above, this is mostly a women's festival. Just as on Dasehra day, the men present each other with leaves of shami tree (which is considered as veritable 'gold'), with the idea of creating friendship or cementing more strongly their already existing friendships; so on this day, women give each other til with the same purpose in view. Fruits and vegetable of the season are also exchanged. Men too similarly exchange til with their men friends.

But before we proceed further, let us see who or what is Sankrant. Sankrant is believed to be a goddess, having large and protruding eyes, loose and long hair, and wearing a long flowing garb made of one piece, of one material, and of one colour. According to the astrologers, every year on this day, at a given time, she passes in flight from one quarter of the earth to the other, say, from north to south or *vice versa*, or west to east or *vice versa*. Every year the colour of her dress changes ; similarly, the animal on which she rides changes from year to year. I am informed that in the year 1925, she had a white dress on and rode on a tiger; the year before a yellow dress and a donkey to ride upon ; and so on. It is believed that all cloth of the colour which she wears in a particular year will be very dear during the year ; and the same is the case with what she eats—grains and fruits, etc. She is fond of eating wheat, and fruits she does not despise. Moreover, woe be to the quarter towards which she keeps looking while passing from one quarter to the other, and to those who dwell in that quarter. It is her wont to keep gazing in one direction through her entire flight from one corner of the Universe to the other. While going from north to south she may be looking in quite a different direction; she may be looking towards one of the four sides. Hence the great anxiety felt by the people about the direction to which she keeps staring while flying over. It is strongly believed that her glance brings great distress and calamity. Most unfortunately, this year, she looked again towards the west! Poor West, it has had enough of disasters! but the goddess wants excitement and sensation ; and for such things, surely she looked in the right direction when she looked towards the west! Yet no one knows her abode—she goes round the world and back into the place from where she started.

The term 'Sankranti' is sometimes used as a term for a quarrelsome woman who is constantly abusing others loudly, and quarrelling in a great rage, with her hair loose and falling on shoulders, her eyes protruding with anger, and that end of the sari which covers the shoulders hanging down and touching the ground.

On 'Til Sankrant' the men must stay out for a long time, in fact, the whole day, as women go in groups from house to house to see their friends if invited. Generally every woman is invited, and friends are pressed to come and pay a visit which is considered a great honour. It is of course understood that the men-folk cannot stay at home when the wives and the sisters of other people are in. Therefore out of courtesy the men go out, and busy themselves with some thing or other. They manage to pass the time either watching the races—bullock cart races—or cock fighting, wrestling, etc., etc., the younger ones are busy kite-flying. It is at this time in the bazars or in some meeting places, that the men present each other with til. Fruits or other such things are not exchanged. The men bow to each other with folded hands or in any other recognized way and wish each other something good. The tils which the writer was offered by his many friends on this day were mixed with jaggery and made into different kinds of palatable preparations. While some were sugar-coated and made into lumps of different sizes and of different colours—the others were made like doughnuts—they were either made into small balls or were shaped in all sorts of odd designs.

On 'Til Sankrant' the women-folk rise early in the morning, to do all the house-cleaning and scouring of utensils. The daughter-in-law washes the feet of the mother-in-law or of any other elderly lady in the house in order to gain her love. After making any food if required (though most of the things are made the previous day, and on this day nothing is eaten which does not contain til and jaggery, and no fast is kept this day), the women take their bath, oil their hair, put in a few flowers in their hair-knots, and clothe themselves in their prettiest saris; then, adorned with all the ornanents they possess, they leave their houses and go in groups from house to house. A carpet or durrie is spread on the ground (though this is hardly necessary, as the floor is always so clean and so nicely and freshly plastered, that there is absolutely no fear of clothes being soiled) and they sit on it in a circle. They exchange with each other vegetables and fruits of the season, such as carrots, peas, guavas, mangoes, plums, sugarcanes, etc. etc.

The fruits are not exchanged uncovered. As mentioned above, they are put in a new earthenware vessel, and covered with one end of the sari of the giver, and then passed from one cover to the other without being seen by either giver or receiver. Moreover, they are not seen even after the exchange has been effected under the cover of the saris; for they should be taken home covered, and only then disclosed to view. This is supposed to show that the giver and the receiver do not pay any regard as to what the fruits are worth in terms of money, but that they care more for the spirit of friendship in which they are given. They are priceless also; for it is said that the thing in a closed hand (of the contents of which you have no knowledge) may be worth Rs. 1,25,000! In other words it is 'unmol' or priceless.

They present each other with new earthenware vessels, mark each other on the forehead with red powder, wishing 'long life' for each other's husband. Even the young unmarried girls go through the whole ceremony, in anticipation of a coming happy married life. If you watch them sitting there you will see that they are not quiet even for a single second. They are chatting, joking, laughing and coughing loudly, and the young ones add their quota by crying. One observes in that company great joy and happiness.

Now, as all this is going on, quite suddenly a mother gets up and announces that she is going to do her 'chhokri ki lut' (the loot of her girl). All are ready, and the woman who announces this makes her girl stand in the middle of the group, and takes many handfuls of different fruits and lets them fall gently off the head of the girl. The women rush for the fruits so dropped on the ground; and one can imagine the rush, the excitement, the jollity, and the laughs and smiles that result from such an innocent performance. After they have gone through a few of such loots they sit down and then jokes are cracked, and pleasant memories and similar occasions recalled.

When they think it is time that they should move on, they do so and go from house to house until they have paid all the calls, thus new acquaintances are formed, and existing friendship cemented till the day is over. In the evening, particular male friends of the husband are invited for dinner (or more often breakfast) and then all is quiet again.

But darkness does not cover the land without the inevitable Brahmans and beggars being fed. It is in the forenoon that these men go from door to door, with full knowledge of what they will get. At every house they get 'khichri' [rice and dall (pulse) mixed together, fried in clarified butter and then boiled in water until it is evaporated, and seasoned with salt] and 'laddus,' til balls made by mixing til and jaggery. The beggars are just as omnipresent as the Brahmans!

Very recently the author had an occasion to entertain the Mahar women of a locality on Til Sankrant Day. There were present about eighty to a hundred women, who were dressed in their best saris and bedecked with jewels. There were only three men of their caste present to help the author in making the necessary 'bandobast'. The author presided at the function, though ordinarily men are not allowed to come into a group of women observing this festival; in fact, on this occasion those men who also wanted to come in—they had their wives and sisters among them—were turned out summarily by some of the women themselves. After running the gramophone for some time, the calm and serene-looking women immediately fell to talking and laughing loudly, and cracking jokes with each other. After having their fill of laughter and mirth, an elderly woman got up with a glittering brass plate in her hand containing red powder; and from one end started marking the women on their foreheads, rather abruptly and rudely skipping over the widows sitting in the row. Besides this woman, the other women also besmeared each other's cheeks and foreheads with the red powder, always accompanied as they did so by pleasant remarks and wishes. After this, the author had the honour of being garlanded by them with a garland of mogra and rose, intertwined with silvery threads. Having finished this part of the ceremony, about six women were asked to distribute fresh peas, plums, big and small, jaggory and sesamum seeds mixed together, carrots, pods of different vegetables and betel leaves and nuts. One of the distributors was a widow; but no sooner was this noticed than a strong protest was raised against this procedure though not in a rough manner. The poor woman had to sit down and a woman with her husband living like the others was asked to distribute the things. As the things were being distributed the women were busy laughing and cracking jokes among each other. One of the jokes was the asking a young wife her husband's name. Many got after her. She felt extremely shy and certainly nothing could make her mention her husband's name. A Hindu woman not only does not call her husband by name but does not even pronounce it in the presence of others. On account of the nature of the author's work which lay among these women he had to take down their children's fathers' names and it was a job to get the names out of them. They would either cover their faces due to shyness or they would immediately ask some other women or men standing near by to let me know their husbands' names. Ordinarily, on the author's asking the name of a woman's husband, about ten people would immediately volunteer to tell it, because they know that a woman is not expected to mention her husband's name. But not infrequently, many a woman, finding no one of her community within hearing distance, has quietly and shyly pronounced her husband's name!

BASANT PANCHMI.

BASANT Panchmi is celebrated on the fifth day of the moon's phase in the month of Magh. This is considered as the first day of spring, though in North India it is generally quite cold about this time, But it is quite spring-like in the central parts of India and also in the West and in the East.

Basanta means Spring and, according to the story, Madan and Rati, though now considered as the God and Goddess of Love, were originally ordinary human beings. As the story goes, on the first day of spring, Madana and his wife, Rati, had intercourse while in the jungle, instead of waiting till they reached home. The God Shiva, who happened to be strolling about, saw this and becoming angry cursed them, and they were burnt to ashes on the spot. But the God Shiva had promised that Madana would be born as the God Krishna's son. So people still worship Shiva on Basant Panchmi day in order that the fate which came upon Madana and Rati should not befall them, and they promise to behave with self-restraint.

On this day some people also worship Vishnu and in Bengal the day is celebrated as Saraswati Puja day, Saraswati being the Goddess of Learning.

In Maharashtra, this day is reserved for other purposes also. On the first Basant Panchmi of the bride and bridegroom, *i. e.*, on the first Basant Panchmi which follows their wedding, the parents of the two give them yellow coloured clothes. Early in the morning the two rub oil on their bodies and are then wrapped in a dhoti or loin-cloth, and made to sit together in the middle of the courtyard and as the musical band stationed in one corner of the courtyard plays, the sisters of the bride and bride-groom pour warm water over them and give them a bath. There is general merriment both among the relations and neighbours who gather for the occasion. In the Central Provinces and the United Provinces, immediately after the bath the God Shiva and his wife Parbatti are worshipped, while Saraswati is worshipped in Bengal. It may be mentioned that ordinarily Shiva is worshipped with the leaves of the bel tree (*Vilva*), but on this day he should be worshipped with mango flowers, and with ears of wheat also, this being the season for them. In some places they use ears of barley, if this is the common grain grown there. Though ordinarily the newly-wed couple perform this ceremony on their first Basant Panchmi day only, the rich go through it almost every year with music and with pomp and show. The woman who takes such a bath invites her women friends in the afternoon and distributes Haldi (Turmeric) and Kunkma (vermilion powder) and sugar mixed with cocoanut. The women sing together and enjoy themselves.

In North India in the Punjab and the North-West Frontier Province boys and young men wear yellow turbans on the Basant Panchmi day. In schools all the Hindu boys come to school next day with yellow *turbans* on. When the author was in school there, if any one did not come in turban of this colour, he was looked down upon. When the days are cloudy, the flowers are in bloom, the anticipatory warmth of the summer is in sight, and the fields are yellow with 'sarson' flowers, and the nightingales and other spring birds hop from twig to twig, then we say Basant Rut (Spring Season) is come. Though the schools have closed for this day, yet on any other day which is very fine the school may be closed again to allow the boys to enjoy themselves outside. It seemed a waste of time to sit inside in class-rooms when the cries of peacocks were to be heard outside the dull walls of the school building. Happy memories of the author's childhood are connected with this festival.

Except in Bengal, Saraswati Puja is done during the Daserah days, that is, during the first ten days of the month of Aswin. In Bengal the Daserah days are entirely taken up by the Goddess Kali or Durga.

Two days before the Daserah day, a Brahmin is called into the house, who puts the sacred books of the house in a pile and lights a lamp over them and recites some mantras. On the next day he conducts the worship of the same books, with the necessary materials of worship, students taking special part in it. All have to keep fast until the worship is over, including the children who are afraid to displease the goddess, lest they should not be helped in their efforts to attain knowledge and wisdom. On the third day, being the last day of the Daserah days, the pile of books is removed and the worship is considered to be complete. Now this is done to invoke the spirit of Saraswati, the Goddess of Learning, who blesses all who are trying to attain knowledge and learning. She is also called the Goddess of Wisdom and Speech, and is a presiding deity of students. She is the wife of Brahma, the Creator. In worship, a goddess is represented either by her image made of clay or metal or by a metal vessel full of rice and covered over with a cocoanut. Such image or its representation is garlanded with flowers by those assembled for worship.

In South Iudia, on this day a large number of all sorts of toys are placed in a room, and the images of Kali, Saraswati and Lakshmi, the Goddess of Wealth, are placed among them as a mark of self-denial to express their sorrow for sins commitetd by them. Men generally do not take any part in this toy-ceremony. It is mostly done by women and children for nine days and sweets, etc., are distributed to the children. This ceremony is done in addition to the worship of books. In South India married women get presents of clothes, though this is not universally done.

Saraswati Puja is faithfully carried out in almost every part of India because it is so enjoined by the Puranas. The story goes that a good and wise king, Suketu, was defeated by his enemies and when he was exiled, his wife accompanied him. In their hour of adversity a sage, by name Angiras, appeared and advised the king and his wife Suvedi to worship the Goddess Durga. As a result of this worship the queen in due time was blessed with a son who grew up to be a strong and powerful man, so much so that he reconquered his father's lost kingdom. Now the royal couple was advised to worship Durga during the Navaratri (the nine days preceding Daserah); hence the reason of this worship during these days, when people believe that in this way they will get what they desire. Now this Saraswati Puja is really what is called Durga Puja in Bengal and elsewhere and occurs during the autumn. In Bengal the day corresponding to Saraswati Puja is the Sri Panchmi day—the day of the Basant Panchmi, *i.e.*, the fifth of the light half of the month of Magh. On this day reverence is paid to the Goddess of Learning. But schools and colleges are closed this day! An image of the goddess is taken through the streets in procession with singing and music. Such processions start from private houses or temples and the images are taken to a near-by river or stream to be immersed in water. The tendency even of College students to do Saraswati Puja in the college building itself has sometimes been embarrassing. The whole of this day is spent in Kirtan and Bhajan—singing of religious songs with music, and reading from the sacred books. No one is allowed to do any work this day. As usual all Government and other offices are closed, as for many other festivals, and no one is supposed to do any work which is ordinarily done every day of the year—a sort of annual sabbath day. One is not supposed to go even to bazaar. One has to be up early and bathe and then to devote oneself to religious devotion; the goddess is to be worshipped either in one's own home or in a temple where people gather together for the purpose. A fast has to be observed the whole day, to be broken only on the next day.

In parts of Central Provinces, especially in the villages, an image of Saraswati is kept in a niche in every school. It is kept in such a prominent place that boys coming into the class-room in the morning do not forget to bow before it with clasped hands. But recently Ganapati or Ganesh, the elephant-headed God, has come to take precedence in this respect. One has now to make obeisance to him before it is done to Saraswati; whatever else one may do one has to bow before him. So it will not be long before Ganesh usurps Saraswati's place entirely. In village schools where Saraswati still holds her sway boys do not sit down to study until they have said 'Namaskar' to the goddess. The boys are generally entered in the village school on this day— Saraswati Puja day—and the teacher expects 'Dakshina', a fee, or money purported to have been offered to the goddess. It is the teacher's due and he gets it. The village teachers themselves have assured the author that the fee does not exceed more than a few annas. They further say that the vogue of Saraswati Puja at least in the village schools of Central Provinces is becoming less and less and that Ganapati is now being given that honoured position.

Boys purchase new books, new slates and other new things on the Saraswati Puja day, and this is also done on a few other occasions.

SHIVA RATRI.

Shiva Ratri = Night devoted to Shiva.

SHIVA is one of the three greatest gods—Brahma, the Creator; Vishnu, the Preserver; and Shiva, the Destroyer—the last one being naturally the most dreaded of all. He is supposed to have a thousand names, and each one of them has got to be recited while worshipping him. Pashupati (the master of the animal, here meant of oxen), Shiva, Mahadeo, Shankar, Har, Rudra, Bhava, Dhurjatti, Gangadhar (dhar = hold = one who holds), Nil-Kantha (one who has the blue mark on his neck, which he got by drinking poison). Trinetre (three eyes), Vishweshwar (Lord of the Universe), Shambhu, etc., etc., are some of his names. He is called Shiva, the Terrible, the Destroyer. Shiva is worshipped every Monday, though originally this day was fixed for moon worship only. There are two more days in the week, which also are undergoing the same sort of change.

Now, this particular Shiva Ratri called the Maha Shivaratri—the big night of the Shiva, there is one

Shivaratri every month which falls on the 13th of the dark half of a month; but this one comes in the month of Magh. Part of the worship is conducted the same night, but the rest is gone through in the day time on the 14th of the dark half which is the 29th of Magh or one day before Amavasya. This is considered a very holy day. There is a story connected with this festival which is worth recording here as it will give the reader some idea of the greatness of Shiva and also of the way in which his worship is conducted.

An irreligious and wicked hunter, who never meditated on the name of Shiva and whose one thought was that of hunting, started out for the jungle, as usual, with a bow and arrows. This particular day, of which we read the story, was the Maha Shivaratri day. On his way to the jungle he met many pilgrims and worshippers who were going to the temple of Shiva in the jungle. He did not take any notice of them until he himself passed by that temple and heard the worshippers say "Shiva Shiva!" and "Har Har!" Now these two expressions are involutary ejaculations used when some one involuntarily sees an evil thing. The hunter stopped and wondered why the worshippers were using those expressions while actually worshipping the stone in the temple. He pronounced the words, and started again, unconscious of the fact that he was unconsciously uttering the god's name.

Now after some time he came across a tank which was thickly shaded by a bel-tree growing on its bank. In order to hide himself from the animals which might come to drink water at the tank, he climbed up the tree, and in order also to have a clear view of the whole tank in front he broke off small twigs and branches and threw them down so that there might be no obstruction while taking aim. On a branch he hung up his waterbag, from which water fell drop by drop on the 'pindi' or 'linga' below.

Now at the same spot where the wood apple tree was standing Brahma himself had once come down to worship Shiva, and had taken the sand out of the tank and made a 'pindi' or 'linga' out of it. So the 'pindi' was still there, and a bel-tree had come out by the side of it. The hunter, of course, did not know anything about this. He had climbed up only in order to have a clear view of the jungle in front. The twigs and leaves which he had broken off for this purpose fell on the 'pindi' without his knowledge. Now the bel leaves are greatly loved by Shiva—in fact the leaves are the most essential material for his worship. Shiva was being worshipped inadvertently and without the man's knowledge; the result was that his sins were being forgiven as he proceeded with the worship unconsciously. At evening, when a doe came to the water side, he pulled the arrow, but just as he was going to let it go she happened to look at him and said: "Why do you kill me? I have not offended you in any way but if you are bent upon doing so please excuse me and let me go for a short while so that I may bid my husband farewell, for I am married and am faithful to him." He said, "I am afraid you won't come back, and I must have you as my children are hungry; but if you promise that you will return immediately, I shall let you go." She promised this and went away. Now this doe had been a favourite dancing girl of the gods in heaven. Through constant patronage she got very proud with the result that they cursed her and sent down to the earth as a doe. She had, however, after a time, gone and complained to Shiva who had promised that she would again be in heaven some day through an accident to a man on Shivaratri day.

Next came a buck who questioned the hunter of his intentions towards him. He was also given leave to go in order to bid farewell to his wife. The buck was originally a god who had been turned out of heaven on account of his bad character there. Then came a doe who promised to return immediatly after she had fed her kids. This doe and another one who came in last were the friends —sakhis—or the playmates of the first doe in heaven and were condemned to become deers along with their friend.

Now, each deer before getting leave had discoursed on some spiritual matters and one of them had gone to the extent of graduating and appraising the sin of killing. For example, one said :—

The killing of	10 goats =	the killing of	1 ox.
„	100 men =	„	1 brahmin.
„	100 brahmins =	„	1 good woman.
„	100 women =	„	1 preg. woman.
„	10 pregnant women =	„	1 cow.

The hunter's whole night was taken up by such discourses and talks on spiritual matters. In the morning the four turned up as promised but he declined to kill them saying, "You are blessed, how can I kill you after your telling me so many good things, especially after telling me about the sin of taking life."

So the man had been kept awake the whole night—one of the essentials of Shiva's worship; the essentials being the repeating of Shiva's name, worship of 'pindi' with water, bel-leaves, keeping fast, of sitting up the whole night, listening to spiritual talks or reading religious books about Shiva.

As his sins were now forgiven he began to have an intense desire to see God, and as a result of which some say he died immediately and got Moksha, while others say that he lived as a Bhagvata or Sadhu for many years afterwards. The writer is also told that immediately after his craving to see God, Shiva himself came down on an udan

Khatola' or flying cot (aeroplane) and took him up and invested him in heaven with godhood.

On Shivaratri people should keep twenty-four hours' fast—fruits and milk may be taken but serious fast-keepers do not drink even water. Men keep awake the whole night and read or listen to stories about Shiva. So do women; but they generally go off to sleep!

All rise early, bathe and go to the temple. They have to worship three times that day. Men must go to the temple with Dindi, *i.e.*, with cymbals, tom-toms along with men singing in praise of Shiva. Though women too go singing, they are not accompanied by musical instruments.

Worshippers carry with them in brass plates the following materials of worship:—Sandalwood paste, rice, turmeric, red powder, wood apple or bel-leaves, flowers, udbatti, incense, camphor and water.

As soon as they enter into the temple, the Brahmins take charge and instruct them as to the method of worship. They recite the mantras as they drop the leaves on the 'linga', and recite all the names of Shiva. Generally, the women go separately from the men, and worship separately in the temple; but this may not be true in all places.

Though the 'linga',—phallus—has been taken as a symbol of the creative power of Nature, yet the majority of the people cannot be expected to think in this strain, and not one in ten thousand even cares to know about this 'higher meaning'. At the same time, to the minds of the unacquainted the 'linga' does not suggest obscene notions.

Shiva is supposed to be everywhere. His head is in the heavens, his upper body in the space between heaven and earth, his 'linga' in the middle, *i.e.*, on the earth where it is considered very sacred, his feet are in the Pātal, the nether-world. His 'linga' has no beginning and no end as discovered both by Brahma and Vishnu. Both of these were set the task of finding out the end of 'linga'. Some say they were asked to find the head and the feet of Shiva respectively. Brahma rode upon his swan and flew up to heaven and Vishnu went down to the nether-world upon his tortoise. While Vishnu told the truth about his inability to find the end, Brahma lied and said that he had found it and brought the Ketki flower, declaring it was fixed on the tip of it. So Vishnu was blessed and invested with new rights and previleges; Brahma was cursed and was declared un-worshippable.

It is commonly believed in the Maharashtra that, from Shivratri the day increase 'shivl by shivl' as from Til Sankrat it increases til by til (= minute oil seed). Shivl is the peg which is fixed in the yoke of an oxen team to keep their heads from slipping out.

The low caste people who have no temples of their own have to worship Shiva at home. The author saw a well-to-do low caste Hindu worshipping in an enclosure made by four cots. Inside he had made a tiny Pindal—a sort of raised ground —surrounded on four sides with strings of fresh mango leaves. It had a tiny gate also. In front of it five leaves were hung apart; underneath each of them was placed one earthenware saucer, one earthenware lamp burning clarified butter, half a cocoanut and then there were flowers and garlands. He had beside him a big brass plate containing food prepared that morning. Rice, dal (pulse), good preparations made of flour fried in ghee—sweet and salty—two kinds of vegetables. He would put in the different saucers a little quantity of the contents and then bow before them with folded hands and shout "Har bolo" and two or three members of his family inside the enclosure along with the spectators standing all around the cots would shout in response in a most religious manner "Mahadeo". (Har = another name for Shiva, bolo = speak.) Mahadeo also is one of Shiva's names. He would ask them to shout the god's names after every such action, and tho youngsters standing all round would never lag behind in shouting at the top of their voices in responso to his requests. The man had arranged before him six pieces of stone, five arranged in a straight line and one opposite to the line. The man on being asked could not account for the stones, nor any one of the others who were standing all round the cots; though he did say that the stone placed separately represents Kala Kotwal (=the black watchman) or Bhairva. He could not say who or what he was, some remarked that people were afraid of him.

After the worship was over, the man broke the half cocoanut into pieces and distributed to the youngsters and women standing around.

They accepted it most reverently and ate it. After it he dismantled the temporary temple and got up.

The most curious thing the author observed during the worship was that the man was not at all serious. He was laughing and smiling, talking to the on-lookers, answering the author's enquiries that were addressed to the people standing about: and he would abuse the boys roundly if, on account of the rush behind, they happened to push or shake the cots a little; and he would use, to the great amusement of all, the name of Mahadeo and his 'linga' in an unpleasantly suggestive manner. He was performing this worship on the morning after the Shivaratri.

In many of the villages of the Punjab and the U. P. one may find small chest-like tiny houses on the roadside or outside the village or near the common well (in many places much bigger also) containing within them either the images of lingas or broken, raised and embossed, shapeless figures (coloured red) and if asked, people will describe them as 'Mahadeo ka thara' or 'Mahadeo ka asthan' (the place, or temple of the Mahadeo).

Outside on the wall one may find painted the figure of a bull. The bull is the animal on which he usually rides.

HOLI

THE Holi (Holika or Hut asani) a very popular festival, falls on the full-moon of Phalgun. Its origin is explained by different men in different ways. Some say that it is a relic of an old Aryan festival and is connected with sun-worship or fire-worship. Others think that it had its origin in the setting aside by the vulgar crowd of a few days for licentious indulgence.

The Hindu religious books also mention a tradition of observing the Holi festival on the full-moon day of this month. There is a legend connected with the festival, that the God of Love was once sent by the gods to Shiva to lodge a complaint against a demon who was troubling them. This poor god went to Shiva at a time when he was busy with his devotions. His wrath at the interruption was so great that the gods' representative was burnt to ashes on the spot. But why this incident is connected with the perpetuation of this festival, perhaps Shiva alone knows.

The following story is also associated with the Holi festival. By virtue of a boon obtained through the favour of Shiva, a demoness by name Holika, became very powerful in a certain town. Besides eating up the children of the locality she began to trouble the people without any apparent cause. They approached Vasishta, a Brahman Rishi (sage), who suggested a way of getting rid of her. On the 15th day of the moon of Phalgun, *i.e.*, on full-moon day, an image of this demoness was to be thrown into the fire, and the burning fuel caught in the hands, and great noise made. At the same time, they were to say all sorts of bad things against her character and organize a sham chase after her, the idea being to annoy her so much that she might commit suicide. As the suggested remedy proved effective, the people kept up the practice till it reached the dimensions it has now assumed. Now the belief is that the troubles and anxieties of the people are thrown into the fire in the form of a demoness, which makes the people happy.

But 'the man in the street' hardly cares to know anything about its origin. Many of the educated Hindus with whom the author has talked, say that the origin was the sun-worship, and that ignorant people have adapted it to their own whims and fancies.

In North India where it is very cold in the winter, people welcome the Holi days as the forerunners of a warmer season though the author knows from personal experience in the North and North-West India that some years it is very very cold during the Holi days—piercing and biting winds blow and the weather is generally very dull indeed.

In the Central Provinces where the summer comes much earlier, people think that the real summer—intense heat—begins from the Holi days and they, no wonder, do not welcome the Holi in the same sense as people do in North India. It has been noticed that it rains fairly regularly on Holi days in Central Provinces also which makes the weather fine and pleasant.

It may be mentioned here that some people take the Purnima (the full-moon day) as the first day of Holi and some as the last day of the five days of the festival.

Fifteen days previous to Holi people begin to make preparations for the burning of a bonfire. Boys and young men go about from door to door begging money for purchasing fuel but particularly to enjoy a feast after the full-moon. In some places in North India, school children go about begging in groups under the personal supervision of their teachers, dancing with small sticks in their hands; but round about Central India this peculiar dance is confined chiefly to the low castes, especially Mahars. After all the begging is done, the regular stealing of things which can be burnt is begun, and the boys steal anything they can lay their hands upon, including crude furniture of any kind, fuel, cowdung, the tearing of door-posts and doors off their hinges is not an uncommon practice. Once in a certain place, all the municipal notice boards disappeared in one night! Shopkeepers are too clever to leave their sign boards over night unguarded. The stolen wooden cots make excellent fuel that day. Bullock carts go the same way. School benches, tables and other furniture have also been seen to be burning on the same pile.

If a tree is lying fallen down on the roadside, a group of boys will go and set fire to it. Wooden things are very unsafe these days. A year ago, the author saw an urchin go up to a bullock cart carrying firewood and without paying any regard to the feelings of the owner-driver began taking out a couple of logs. When in great anger the driver wanted to know what he was doing, the boy without caring to lift up his eyes, simply and very calmly replied, "Don't you know it is Holi?" The wonder of wonder is that he did not say a word and the boy coolly went away with two decent-looking logs.

The whole atmosphere that day is charged with a peculiar madness. Boys often go beyond the limits of decency.

Once, an accomplice in a Holi day adventure told the author that he, along with a few other boys of the locality, entered the house of a newly married couple, rather late at night and very cautiously lifted their beds, and brought them fast asleep to the Holi fire in the street where previously strict silence was enjoined and was observed. It was the old man's third marriage. No sooner had they dropped the cots to the ground abruptly than the couple, in the midst of great noise and mischievous allusions, opened their eyes and for a minute they could hardly tell whether everything that was happening there was real or a dream. The couple looked at each other and then at the crowd and then to the sky and the stars and then to the fire which reminded them of the Holi and the possibilities connected with it. The old man was in a furious rage. He began to curse them most profusely, all the more so when their bed-clothing was thrown away at a safe distance from the fire, and the cots themselves into the fire. The bride ran away to her home and the old man followed suit on realizng his utter helplessness.

Holi is an occasion on which the suppressed scandal of the previous year is publicly announced without any restrictions, and always to the face and in the presence of the person or persons connected with it. It is a pathetic sight if a victim, whether a man or a woman, passes by the crowd of the Holikars. The leading man of the group asks in a loud voice a meaningful question of the crowd in regard to the victim who is passing by, and they in reply shout out at the top of their voices giving in the minutest details the whole scandal. In return the victim gets angry but has to run away as there is no other recourse. Young women, as a rule, are not allowed to go out during those days and they are strictly prohibited by their parents, husbands or brothers to even peep out of their house doors, because a mere sight of a girl might bring forth abusive language from Holi-walas. An old man generally makes a very good victim, because he is reminded of the scandal of his young days without regard being had to the fact that he has now perhaps renounced the world and is busy in his religious pursuits. The wrath of the old man can better be imagined than described. He showers a volley of abuses on the young men but that of course acts like drops of water on an oily surface. If a person cannot take revenge on any other day of the year, this is the day.

It has been described above how the necessary fuel is collected for the Holi bonfire. Now on the Holi day all the stolen fuel is piled in a place and in the centre of it a plant of Shevar (*Seskami alzytia*) is fixed failing to get this plant they use castor or *arandi* plant as substitute. Some times a red or green flag is substituted. The origin of the fixing of the plant is not known but is followed as an old custom. After the time of the burning of the Holi is announced, the young people busy themselves with Pakwans and other eatable preparations until the evening draws nigh when a drum is beaten with a peculiar and special beat to call the people from their houses to a place where the fire is going to be lit. At the appointed time people gather round the pile and throw on it some of their own fuel which they bring from home and set fire to. The ordinary process of worship of the pile is gone through and then it is immediately followed by Bom Thokna. (Bom Thokna means the striking of the back side of the hand against the mouth and producing a loud sound.)

Those who do not want to attend the common Holi because they do not like to indulge in unpleasant fun, burn a Holi at home and worship it there. But they have to fast that day, though others who take part in public bonfire are generally exempt from this.

Holi is not burnt in a single place in a village or a town. Different streets or sections of the town have their own Holis burnt and the same process gone through. It is after the process of Bom Marna that the unpleasant fun described above begins. This goes on till the young men have done all the jumping over the fire though it does not always end there as the young men are not satisfied yet. After the fire is out, the older people go home to break their fast. It is not necessary that all the bonfires should go on the whole night. Though some are kept up the whole night or for a few hours, there are others—not many—which are kept burning for the full fifteen days. After the fires are out, and only ashes are left over, the young girls go immediately and fetch water and pour over the ashes. They take the ashes home and spread it in a circle round about which some plastering is done with cowdung; then an image of Parvati with five horns is made and worshipped according to the prescribed method. This is done in order to gain a good husband. This is done regularly for some 15 days.

This custom of bonfires is like the one that was observed in England of bygone days on Midsummer Day. To leap over the flames was considered beneficial in curing diseases. And on this very day girls would use different devices to discover their future husbands.

Dhurvad follows after the first day and lasts till the 4th day. During this period people come out of their houses, form into parties and throw at each other any dirty thing imaginable—refuse, ashes, pealings of fruits, water and mud, etc. After finishing with themselves they make common cause and wait for the passers-by on whom they throw rubbish. Some of them soak a long piece of cloth in gutter water and lash it on the passers-by. During these three days it is rather dangerous to pass by or under the windows of the houses as at any time anybody may be completely covered with rubbish or ashes. Cautious people generally put on special clothes for the occasion. The author always did so in his boyhood days. In big cities the Holi Festival does not generally pass off peacefully. Almost every year a number of men are arrested by the police on a charge of disorderly conduct, for indiscriminately throwing mud, dye-stuffs, coloured water and cowdung at pedestrians and at passengers in tram cars. Even brickbats and other hard missiles are also used occasionally.

The fifth day is called the Rang-Panchmi—the colour-fifth. This day, coloured water is thrown at each other. It is generally done by means of tin or bamboo syringes. Sham fights between parties are arranged and the party unable to withstand the tremendous flow of coloured water is taken to be defeated. This day the faces of the men are always well-coloured. They soak their hands in some sort of wet colour and rub them on each others faces and the passer-by is not frequently let alone. Boys go about in the streets with a thick plaster of some colour on the palms of their hands. As soon as they see a victim—one whose face is not covered with colour—they spit in their hands to wet the colour and rub it on the face of the victim forcibly. One can't expect them to carry about water to wet their hands on the Holi days, because decency is the thing which for a few days is entirely banished from their minds.

People do not mind drinking if they feel like doing so and this leads them further. Hindu washermen, cobblers and shoemakers drink heavily on this day. They go about the streets singing filthy songs and beating tomtoms, dressed in white shirts sprinkled over with all shades of colour. In a certain town in Central Provinces the Mahars—a low caste—take out what they call a *mel.* They pick out a number of young boys—about 15 years of age—who are dressed in fancy girls' costumes. With drums, harmoniums and flutes they go to the houses of their patrons and friends of higher castes and give exhibition of their dances. They spend quite an amount of money on paints, trinkets and dresses but they are generally able to recover their expenses and enough to enjoy a feast almost every day of the Holi season through the 'bakshish' that they get. Their greatest patron is the Raja who, as they said, is bound to have their dance performed in his palace every year and pay a handsome reward.

On Rang-Panchmi many follow the example of Krishna with the 16,000 Gopies (herdswomen) of Gokul where he was brought up. Rang-Panchmi is played in families too, between sisters, wives of the sons and other ladies of a joint family. On this day the streets are covered with all sorts of colours, the doors and walls are full of them, and almost every Hindu is covered with it from head to foot.

People generally wear old white garments to give them a striking effect.

A traveller in Nepal found that during the Rang-Panchmi day all the streets were coloured green and red and that even the frontier was dyed in a similar manner. There even the ears of both men and women are syringed with coloured water.

Some Brahmins consider the new-born child impure until it has been taken round the Holi-fire thrice in the arms of its mother and the fire worshipped with sprinkling water and by throwing grains and cocoanuts in the fire. Cocoanut rescued from the fire is considered holy and spiritually good for the eater. Some sects of Brahmins sprinkle red Holi powder on the white garment of the child. It is considered purifying.

A child carried round the bonfire seven times is believed to be safe against the attacks of witches.

The iron or wooden pegs with which the household cattle are tied if touched with fresh cowdung taken out of the bonfire is considered a good preventative against the attacks of witches and also diseases of diverse kinds.

Salt bought on Holi day if heated on the bonfire and given to the animals saves them during the year from diseases peculiar to them.

If a Brahmin or any other high caste man on this day touches a low caste man or woman, provided he takes bath immediately after it, is considered immune against all kinds of illnesses.

VARSHPRATIPADA

(Gudhi Padva)

THIS festival falls on the new-moon of the month of Chaitra. Many reasons are given to explain why the Hindu new year begins from this particular day, but they do not seem to be very reliable. Some say it began with the Samvat era of Vikramajit, on the day he returned victorious from his battles; and this seems to be the most favourite theory. Even now it is customary for every family to fly a banner. Others say that the first of Chaitra is appointed to commemorate the coronation day of King Vikramajit. There are still others who say that the erecting of the flag poles is done in honour of Ram's victory over Ravan in Lanka and his return to his home in Ajudhiya. Another reason given is connected with the sage Narad, who on his own request was turned into a woman and to whom were born sixty sons; the birth of first son being marked by the new year day. The Hindu years are grouped in cycles of sixty years, and each year bears a name after one of the sons of Narad. In the Panchanga or the calendar of the Hindu year, each son is supposed to be the guardian of his own year; so there are sixty kinds of Samvats, each bearing the name of one of Narad's sons. Divali marks another New Year's Day which is observed mostly by Vaishya caste—the traders, merchants and money-lenders. Their year is called Samvat, after the name of Raja Vikramajit, and the year mentioned in this chapter belongs to the Saka era, after one Raja Shaliman who founded it in 78 A. D. The Samvat era was instituted in 57 B. C.

All over the country this day is observed in a more or less similar manner, though in Malabar it is attended by music, presentations and feasts. There, people collect their valuable things in a room, especially the precious metals in the shape of coins and jewellery, etc., and burn a few lights, and early in the morning they go in with their eyes shut and open them just when they are in front of the articles, the underlying idea being to see something good on the morn of the very auspicious day of the new year. In other parts of India though people have an early bath, especially the women who must have a bath this day and anoint their hair with oil, there is nothing of special interest in which they indulge. They do not usually care to put on jewellery or even new clothes, though some do. In the Central Provinces specially, nothing extraordinary is done except a little of Puja or worship and the flying of the flag. In Northern India the flying of flag has not been noticed, nor is this done in South India; but it is mostly done in the Maharashtra, Gujrat and Kathiavar.

In the Central Provinces the festival is observed as follows: The pole is first washed and then besmeared with red powder and turmeric. On its top end is tied a piece of new cloth or a woman's Choli (bodice or blouse). On the top of the flag they hang a garland of mango leaves, or of flowers, or of toys made of sugar and the top also supports an inverted lota—a glittering vessel of copper or brass. This metal vessel has no particular significance. This is done to take the place of the glittering top end of a royal banner. This pole is placed outside the house door very early in the morning supported by the wall, or tied to a tree or thrust through a hole. The ground under the pole is previously plastered over with cowdung. This is marked with white powdered chalk in all sorts of designs, in certain cases they look so minutely and carefully done that one would wonder as to the length of time they must have taken to do. So on this ground is placed a small tripod, which is kept attached to the pole. On this is arranged the different material of worship, such as the paste of sandalwood, soaked raw rice, flowers, leaves, of wood-apple tree, incense, red powder, the fragrant black powder, turmeric, Kunku (red powder used by women for marking their foreheads), sugar and ghee, mixed and placed on a leaf or in a brass utensil. The worshipper takes these things one by one and throws a small quantity of each on the pole and for every material he throws on it he mumbles that he worships the god with this (the name of the material). These are the ŏnly mantras which are used and do not require the help of a Brahmin. On the tripod are placed also delicious eatables, specially prepared for the day. After making oblations of water, the eatables are distributed among the family members. As soon as the worship is over the children of the family busy themselves with the eatables, and there is general merriment all round. It may be mentioned in passing that such oblations of water are made every time a Hindu takes a meal. Water is taken in hand and thrown on the ground round the utensil containing food. This is done to signify that the food was offered first to God and thus the person taking food considers it the 'left over' of God, and is happy to have His jhuta or the 'left over', and considers it an honour. It is akin to saying grace among Christians.

Among a certain section of the people it is customary to eat the bitter leaves of nim tree. The leaves of this tree eaten this day are believed to protect from Mata (small-pox) and the goddess of this disease Mata or Sitla Devi is thus propitiated for the year. In India the leaves of nim tree are commonly used for medicinal purposes. As observed in the Central Provinces, if one contracts small-pox, the women folk of the family collect other women of the locality or her own female relations, without delay and set out to a temple to propitiate the goddess in order to seek her merciful attention on the victim. They go singing the praises of the goddess of small-pox, carrying on their heads brass vessels full of water and twigs of nim (*Melia*) tree thrown in them. These twigs are placed in front of her image or before a red coloured stone representing her. They return home singing and no effort is made to have recourse to medicines or other help of the kind. But recently people have begun to get themselves vaccinated in large numbers in spite of the prejudice of many people against it. A section of Mahar community have quite a curious idea about the whole question of vaccination. They say that the real object in exhorting people to get vaccinated is different from that of the immunity against small-pox. They think that by scratching the skin of a person the Governmant in reality wants to know whether he or she will remain a loyal subject of it or not. If by scratching blood comes out, the person shall ever remain loyal, and if milk comes out, the Government takes all precautions as he or she is their potential enemy and might create a revolution!

This has, however, been a digression. It may be mentioned that the new year day is considered to be very auspicious for any new venture such as the opening of a shop or starting a business concern, or sending a boy to school for the first time. They wait for this day for such purposes. This being the first day of the year, people engross themselves in religious practices and give alms to the poor. In fact the whole day is passed in the thought as to whether the year is going to be an auspicious one or not, and for this purpose they consult 'jotshis' (astrologers); and if they discourage farmers about the prospect of their crops and traders in their business by giving an unfavourable forecast of the ensuing season, or predicting some calamity, their victims work half-heartedly, although the forecast generally does not come true in the end. Women and poor and ignorant people have great faith in them. On this day they generally get together in a temple and ask all sorts of questions of the astrologer who for every question asks the questioners to place different kinds of coins on different pages of his book of astrology. He will ask for a silver rupee to be placed in one place and a piece of gold to be placed on another and copper in a third place and nickel coins on the fourth till he thinks that he has safely reached the maximum limit of the paying capacity of the questioner. Educated people do not have much faith in them except for the sake of amusement they will call a passing man of the tribe and pay him an anna or two.

People in these days do not ask such questions as were asked by people living in independent Hindu kingdoms, or during the time of the Muhammedan rule in India. For instance, who was going to be the Ruling King of the year, or his minister, whether the year was going to be a bad or a good one; forecast about the rains and the weather in general; who was going to be the presiding god of the year; what would be the proportion of good or bad during the year, etc. Women have generally many private questions to ask and they can easily get hold of an astrologer on that day. They instinctively put out their hands to be read and it is of course always well read as there is nothing read to discourage them with the result that the palmist also goes away happy, loaded with all they are capable to give in Bakhshish.

Some people collect in a place and ask some Brahmin to read to them the almanack or calendar of the year. This booklet called Panchanga from which he reads, can be had from bazaar for an anna or so and those who are literate read it for themselves.

RAMNAUMI

DASRATH, king of Ajudhia, had three wives, Kausaliya, Kaikaie and Sumitra. Ram, Kausaliya's son, was the eldest; Laxman, Sumitra's son, the second; Bharat, Kaikaie's son, the third and Shatruguna, Sumitra's second son, was the youngest.

Once king Dasrath went out to battle against a neighbouring king and took Kaikaie along in his chariot, she being the youngest of the wives. In the heat of the battle when the king himself was shooting arrow after arrow and the chariot was reeling to and fro, Kaikaie noticed that one of the wheels was just going to drop off, the spike holding the wheel having slipped out. She put her own hand into the place and kept the wheel from falling off. As the king happened to look back after the victory he realized to his amazement what she had been doing. He was so greatly struck by her fidelity that he promised her any two boons which she might ask, and which when she did eventually ask placed him in an awkward situation. The story of the boons is given below:—

One night Dasrath dreamed that he would commit three great sins in one day. He stated it to his guru Vashishta who did not show much surprise at it as he knew that Ram, one of the incarnations of Vishnu, was to be born in the f ily, who would be exiled for fourteen years, and consoled the king by saying that he should not worry about it.

One day Dasrath went out for shikar—hunting—and sat by a tank to await some animal who might come down thither to drink water. At a distance he saw a boy (whose name was Shrawan) carrying a Bahngi—a big balance like contrivance for carrying things. The boy carried his old and blind parents in each basket and was bound for Kashi (Benares) on pilgrimage. The older people always have a great desire to visit it before death. As they were thirsty and wanted water, he hung the *bahngi* on to a tree in order that they might be safe from wild animals and went to the tank to fill the lota (vessel with narrow neck) with water. Now Dasrath had not seen the boy going down, so when he heard the gurgling sound of the water going into the narrow mouth of the vessel, he took aim and let fly an arrow in the direction of the sound, (being unable to see on account of thick growth all round) thinking that some animal had come down to drink water. He heard the scream of the boy and ran down to see what he had done. The boy had been struck right in the heart and was crying 'Hai Ram, Hai Ram'; and on enquiry explained his presence there. He asked Dasrath to give his thirsty parents some water to drink and immediately after breathed his last. Dasrath took them water with no intention to speak lest they should recognize his voice and question about their son. But the parents insisted on asking him his reasons for being so late when he knew that they were so thirsty. The king had to explain the whole thing and on account of intense grief, the old people died immediately, crying for Shravan and cursing the king that he would also die crying for his children. Thus he was instrumental in killing three persons during one day. He recited the story to Vaishishta but was quite happy in one way and that was because thereby as a result of the curse he was sure to get children, as until then he had no children and was longing for some, though he knew that by the curse of Shravan's parents they were to die as also by curse they were to be born. In due time Kausaliya conceived and before giving birth she once got frightened and exclaimed "Where is my arrow. I want to kill Rawan". The people around got frightened and quostioned Vaishishta who said that there was nothing to be surprised at as this was to happen as ordained. It may be mentioned here that Ravan, king of Lanka (Ceylon), who know that he would be killed by the hands of Ram, tho son of Kausalya, had put Kausalya when yet a girl in a box and thrown away in the sea in order to destroy her but unfortunately for Ravan the box had been washed ashore and rescued.

Ram was born in due time and when he was grown up, Dasrath decided to abdicate in favour of his eldest son—Ram. Now Kaikaie had a servant woman by name Manthara. She instigated Kaikaie against Ram and reminded her of Dasrath's promise of granting her any two boons she wanted. She said that it was the time and advised her to ask for 14 years of exile for Ram and the throne for Bharat, her own son. Kaikaie went in mourning when she saw that preparations were being made for giving the throne to Ram and thus with her womanish cunning and with the king's promise she managed to get what she wanted though the king was very sad that such things should have been asked by Kaikaie whom he considered a good woman. However, when Ram came to know of it, he readily consented and said that Kaikaie too being his mother, he would go to the jungles for fourteen years. Bharat was at this time at his uncle's. When he returned he found what his mother had done. He became very angry and said where there was no Ram—an incarnation of God Vishnu himself—there was no place for him to live. Bharat loved Ram dearly and could not tolerate this separation. He left everything and put Ram's slippers on the throne and disappeared in the jungles to pass his days in voluntary exile. Kaikaie now regretted very much and was very sad over the whole affair. However, Ram left for the jungle accompanied by his wife Sita and brother Laxman. The Government was carried on by ministers.

After fourteen years, Ram reached Lanka (Ceylon) where he killed the giant king Ravan who had stolen away his wife Sita while in the jungles. He put his (Ravan's) brother Bhibishan on the throne of Lanka and returned with Sita. Bhibishan was very fond of Ram and considered himself his devotee. On her release Ram suspected Sita's purity of character and on the suggestion of Sita herself he put her in a furnace to test whether she had preserved her honour while in the palace of Ravan. She came out unscathed and lived happily with him until one day in order to find out as to what people thought of him on account of taking Sita again as his wife after her return from Ravan's palace at Lanka, he deputed a man to inform him of all that he would hear in this connection. That man not many days after heard a Dhobi (washerman-low caste) refusing, within the hearing of the neighbours, to take back his wife into his house after her living away from him for a month or so in the house of her own parents and declaring questioningly and tauntingly that he was not Ram that he should admit his wife into the house after her long (?) absence from his home. When Ram heard of this taunt, he at once turned Sita out into the jungles where she gave birth to twins whose names were Lahoo and Kush.

Now in the olden days it was a custom among the powerful kings to let loose a fully caprisoned horse to roam about at large which no one dared capture unless with the intention of declaring war against the king to whom the horse belonged. The roamings of the horse at large, in a rough manner described the boundaries of the kingdom. Ram's two sons once caught the horse and did not let him go with the result that the father had to fight with his forces against his two children who were just two, with no force. Ram was defeated and after a time was reconciled to his children.

So Ramnaumi is observed on the ninth day of the month of Chait in honour of the birth of Ram. For eight days previous to this Ramayan is recited in a singsong manner by a Haridasi (the servant of god) before a large audience every day till on the 9th noon exactly at 12 o'clock he stops, this being the time at which Ram is said to have been born. This Haridasi recites the history of Ram, the purpose of his birth, etc. He sings about ten verses and then stops to explain to the audience the meaning of the verses with suitable comments of his own and so on. This man being professional, acquires a certain degree of skill which is necessary to produce the desired effect. Such kirtans are generally held in the compound of a temple. At 12 o'clock noon (12 o'clock at night in the case of Krishna who was born at midnight) the Haridasi announces the birth of Ram and takes a doll, wooden or made of cloth and nicely decorated, and puts it in a cradle and rocks it, and no sooner is it done than the people gathered together in the compound begin throwing Gulal (Red powder) on the cradle to express their joy, while a man takes a brass tray with a small quantity of Gulal in it and goes round to mark the forehead of each one of the audience; the musical band already stationed outside the garlanded gate (with strings of fresh mango leaves or plantain leaves or garlands of flowers) of the temple immediately begins .playing and there is a great hustle and bustle in and outside the temple, crackers and rockets adding to the din. People distribute Parsad—sacrament—and sweets and fruits among the audience. Some distribute curd mixed with sugar and slices of banana fruits,

A fast must be observed that day up till the birth of Ram at 12 o'clock and generally people do not sleep that night. As ordinarily in the house where a child is born, the man and other members of the family hardly get any time to take their meals, so it has become a sort of tradition to observe a fast till 12 o'clock; it is probably not enjoined. People this day worship the images of Ram, Sita and his faithful brother Laxman with mantras, others worship the Ramayan book, and on the same day or the day following, the silver images of them are taken through bazars with music. This is an enjoyable sight. The cars in which these images are taken are beautifully decorated and look dainty. In some places, in place of these images three boys dressed to represent Ram, Sita and Laxman are taken through the bazars with all the Eastern splendour. The image of Maruti—the Monkey god is also carried on chariots in procession along with Ram and others. He is considered to be god Ram's carriage just as other gods have their own animals for carrying them about. It was Mauruti who helped Ram in burning Lanka and it was he who carried a whole mountain when Ram wanted him to bring a particular herb from a certain mountain.

Every one observes this day and celebrates it with as much rejoicings and feastings as possible, because by observing the birthday of god Ram, the sins of the worshippers are washed as white as snow. In Northern India Ram stands more or less for God. A common way of salutation among Hindus is just to say "Ram Ram" meaning may Ram be praised. "Ram Ram." is used also to ejaculate an expression of abhorrence towards a thing, meaning 'O Ram save us', or 'take the name of Ram' and do'nt do such a thing, etc.

In the Central Provinces. the Hindus go to a place of pilgrimage called Ramtek, about twenty miles from Nagpur. 'Ramtek' means the place where

Ram on his way back from Ceylon halted for a time accompanied by his wife Sita. There a temple is situated on the top of a hill reached by scores of steps. Here a fair is held every year and people come from far and near. The low caste Hindus—Mahars and others—are not allowed to enter the temple but they can worship the image from a distance and the material of worsaip such as flowers and cocoanuts they deposit on the steps only. A little distance away from the temple is a small pit or a tank in which Sita is said to have taken bath and that place also is worshipped every year. A worshipper pays a pice for a tea spoonful of this water. He rubs it on his forehead.

Feasting of Brahmins and friends is done on the second day of Ramnaumi when in the morning the women of the house sprinkle the ground with water in front of their houses and with powdered chalk make excellent designs on them—flowers, religious symbols, or anything which they like to have an outline of. The women take great pride in the designs they make.

Before closing the chapter it may be mentioned that Sita is considered an ideal of Indian womanhood for devotion to husband in trials and tribulations and for faithfulness amidst temptations.

Ram may be recognized by his four hands, each holding a couch shell, a discus, a club with a thick end and a lotus flower; like Krishna he also had blue complexion.

In the Central Provinces the author once saw two processions going to a tank on Ramnaumi day. One belonged to Hindus from the United Provinces— and the other to the Sweepers. In the one belonging to the high caste Hindus there were about thirty women, fifteen of whom carried on their heads small earthenwares containing very thick growth of yellowish wheat sprouts for which seeds had been sown about ten days previous to the festival. The sprouts led one to think of very nature sprouting in all its glory. It was about the middle of April. These sprouts gave the idea of something new and newly born—this being the aniversary of Ram's birth. In the middle of the sprouts some had a brass utensil of narrow neck round which was wound a garland of white flowers and on top of it a capsule burning a wick in clarified butter, surrounded by raw green limes. At the head of the procession was a group of men with tom tom and cymbols singing hymns in praise of mother Kali. In the middle of this group, of men in the front and the group of women behind, there were three men whose cheeks were pierced through and through by long iron tridents. The other ends of these tridents—each about 6 ft. in length—were supported by three men who kept them in level with the cheeks in order to give the pierced men as much relief as possible.

The end of the trident which came out on the other side of the men's cheeks was covered by a packet of Pan (beetle leave) of tringular shape. These men whose cheeks were pierced through were walking very quietly, though they were considered to be possessed of Kali Mata. At every stop a man would cut a lime into two and would press them each by hand, right in front of these men, quite near their faces. As was told to the author, the pressing of the cut limes in front of those men was a sacrifice performed in lieu of goats and other animals. As mentioned above these men were at that time considered to be possessed of the goddess. This procession reached a big tank where the tridents were taken out of the men's cheeks and the pots containing wheat sprouts were thrown in the tank and of course not the sprouts themselves. They were washed and brought back and distributed among friends and relatives as tokens of greetings.

The procession of sweepers was not different from that of the Hindus except in a few details. In this men carried the sprouts in the form of torch lights while women had tiny red flags in pots placed in the midst of sprouts on their heads. The women and men were dressed in their best clothes and the procession had the usual formation—men and a singing party with a priest in front and women in the rear. In between them there was a young man whose one cheek only was pierced by a long iron trident. In the middle of the trident was a solitary cocoanut pierced through previously. This young man was also considered to be possessed of mother Kali. He constantly kept dancing a dance which looked more like the shivering of the body. This procession also terminated at the tank. On enquiry from the sweepers the author found that they made no distinction between Ram and Kali Mata. They said that it was all one, both being gods. Most of the sweepers did not know at all as to why they did the whole thing except that it was a Ramnaumi day. After their return from the tank they sacrificed a goat in front of the image of Kali.

HANUMAN JAIANTI.

ON the full moon of the month of Chaitra, the first month of the Hindu Calendar, is observed the birthday of Hanuman, the monkey-god. He is called Maruti also, and is worshipped all over India. In some places he has been given special temples where his devotees are regular worshippers. Wherever there is a temple of Ram, there Hanuman's image is sure to be somewhere near him ; in processions where Ram and Sita are carried, Hanuman is not absent. In North India—in Amritsar, Lahore and on the Frontier—where the effigy of Ravan, the king of Ceylon, is burnt, it is the job of Hanuman to come jumping along and set fire to it. This is due to the well-known story that it was he who was instrumental in securing Sita's release from the demon-king. Hanuman jumped from India to Ceylon and found Sita. When Ram conducted a war against this king, he built a bridge of rocks to enable the forces of Ram to cross in safety. It may be mentioned that in the sea between India and Ceylon there are many rocks. Hanuman set fire to Lanka (Ceylon) and returned with Ram to Ajudhiya. Once Ram asked him to bring a particular herb from a mountain. As he did not know which particular herb he wanted, he carried the whole mountain on the palm of his hand and brought it to Ram to pluck one for himself. Pictures of this scene are commonly found in Hindu homes.

As a result of Hanuman's proving so useful to Ram and Sita, monkeys in many cities are allowed to live freely about the temples; and not only this, but the whole town is infested with monkeys, who are bold enough to snatch things from one's very hands without the least ceremony. In small towns they are a pest. They generally live on the roofs of the houses of the town and they are ever ready as they keep peering into the rooms below to take away any thing—whether eatables or pieces of cloth. Yet no one is allowed to shoot them or molest them in any way. They will lay their hands upon anything; costly sarees and blouses, ordinary clothes and rags, all come alike to them. They will take away a piece of cloth and seat themselves very comfortably in one corner of the roof, every moment expecting the owner to come up and beg for it. And the poor owner knows what to do. He (or generally she) will bring a bit of some chapati and coax the monkey to leave the cloth and take the bit af chapati. Ordinarily, they are amenable to reasonable request, as has been the experience of the author for about 12 years.

If you won't give them some food, they will tear the cloth strip by strip as if to give you enough time to make up your mind to feed them with something.

The monkeys that are allowed to roam about in the towns are like spoiled children. They insist on having what they want, and they get it; and as a result the people suffer a great deal. The author has often heard women crying for their gold necklaces and other jewellery picked up by the monkeys from inside the house and thrown away in the streets and on roofs of the houses, broken in pieces. Poor children avoid passing the very lanes round about which the monkeys habitually spend their time in the morning or the afternoon. The author himself once jumped from the roof of his house when attacked by a bunch of them.

A picture which is also commonly met with in Hindu homes is that of Hanuman trying apparently to reach the sky. The picture depicts his jump to attack Rahu the demon, who was trying to swallow the sun. The reason that he did so was that when Hanuman was born he saw the sun in the early morning and taking it to be some red-coloured, delicious fruit he jumped from his bed to snatch it as is the wont of his progeny unto this day. It was during the making of this effort that he realized that the sun was being swallowed by Rahu whom he threw back with sufficient force to disable him for at least one year, *i.e.*, till the next eclipse of the sun.

The worship of this monkey-god is either conducted in temples or in the homes with the help of small images or pictures. On his birthday the monkeys have 'the time of their life', at least once a year, when they are not only fed sumptuously, but women and even men bow before them with clasped hands, with loud 'namaskars' and other words of respect!

AKSHYA TRITIYA.

THE ceremony peculiar to this day, if performed three days before Chaitra the 30th (in the dark half) is called Pitru Amavas; otherwise the proper date is Vaisakh Shudh the third, *i.e.*, on the third of the light half of the month of Vaisakh. In the Central Provinces, people perform this ceremony either on the Pitru Amavas, or on the Akshya Tritiya day itself, which is the proper day. 'Akshya' = imperishable, permanent, stationary; 'Tritiya' = third. Vaisakh Shudh the third is the day when Sat Jug or Satya Yuga—the Period of Truth—began, and this day is kept as the anniversary. In Hindu mythology, it is the day of the beginning of our world; and the end is not far away, for we are living in Kaliyuga, the age of corruption and of sin, injustice, and infidelity; even the man in the street is well acquainted with this yuga. When he affirms that tho world is in a bad way, he says: "it is no wonder, for we are living in Kaliyuga"; as if men are not responsible for their conduct and are helpless in the matter and it is the times that are to answer in the sight of God, for the daily life of human beings!

Vaisakh Shudh the third is the anniversary of the day when the Satya Yuga began; but in the Central Provinces or in Maharashtra, Akshya Tritiya is observed as the anniversary day of Tretiya Yuga.

Before proceeding to record how the Akshya Tritiya is actually observed by the common people, it would be well to say something about Parasrama (Rama-with-the-axe). He was a Brahmin by caste, and son of the sage Jamadagni. He killed his mother Renuka for her sinful life, though she was restored to life and purified by her husband. The son was blessed with long life for killing a sinner.

Parasrama's one object in life was to clear the earth of the Kshatriyas. He got his chance once when their king raided the forest dwelling of a sage and made his worship impossible by carrying away the calf of the cow whose milk he used to use in his worship. The sage took revenge by killing him. The sage in turn was killed by the king's son. Parasrama therefore rose in great wrath and cleared the Kshatriyas off the face of the earth.

There is another version of the struggle of Parasrama against the Kshatriyas. It is said that with his axe he cut off the arms of one Rajah Sahasrabahu (Sahasra = 1,000, Bahu = Arms) twenty-one times, and every time they immediately grew up again though eventually the Rajah died. Including these twenty-one fights Parasram defeated the

Kshatriyas altogether thirty-six times, and it was at the thirty-seventh time that he himself was defeated and consequently retired honourably into the Mahendra mountain, where he still lives as the patron God of the Chitpavan Brahmins.

Another story is, that when in the Court of Rajah Janak, where the great princes and kings, including Ravan, the king of Lanka, had gathered together to try their luck for the hand of Sita, his daughter, Ravan seeing that Ramchandra had broken the bow—the condition of gaining the hand of Sita—out of jealousy, induced Parasrama to fight with Ramchandra; but Shiva, the Mahadeo, in the meantime handed over a Dhanus (a bow) to Parasrama to challenge Ramchandra to string it (it requires a great deal of strength to string a big, thick bow) saying that if he did so, Parasrama must consider himself defeated for the first and the last time and admit Ramchandra as an Avatar or incarnation of God (Vishnu). Ramchandra, however, accepted the challenge and accomplished the task quickly and Parasrama had to retire from the field.

There is yet another story which shows the importance of Vaisakh the third. Bhagirath, a Kahatriya king, wanted to get all his relatives absolved from sin, and as he knew that his relatives had neither the courage nor the strength to do penance for their own salvation, he undertook on himself to do all the necessary penance on their behalf, in order to excite the admiration or pity of the God to send down the river Ganges for the purpose of enabling the relatives to bathe in it and get absolved, and thus saved from their sins. So according to his determination he underwent twelve years' long and rigorous penance, and sent up his prayers and supplications to God Shiva in heaven, who eventually did take pity on him, and heard his prayers. As Shiva knew that Bhagirath would not be able to stand the tremendous flow of the river on his head he himself came down from heaven and received the river on the long hair of his head, from which it flowed down to earth.

In common parlance, the name of Bhagirath is generally brought in as an example of one who makes tenacious efforts. His name is symbolic of tenacity and determination.

On this day people invite Brahmins and feed them with the choicest food, and also give them fans, earthernwares, shoes, cloth, a little money and the fruits of the season, in order to get the same favours at the hands of the gods, when they themselves depart for the heavens on their death. So it was on Vaisakh Shudh the third, that the Ganges was brought to earth from heaven; and that is why generally people go and bathe in the Ganga; because they commonly believe that their sins are forgiven by simply taking a bath in the river. This day, moreover, is considered a very auspicious one.

Pilgrims who return after taking an ashnan (bath) in the Ganga bring along with them bottles and even pitchers filled with water, nicely sealed up, in order that not a single drop of the precious contents may be wasted. The young bride keeps it in a bottle in her wedding clothes, and regards it as precious as her jewellery, nay more than that. She would rather loose her clothes or jewellery, than the 'Ganga Jali'— the water of Ganga. It is generally kept in a niche, above the reach of children's hands, or stored away in a box under lock and key. It is kept in the house for its own sake, being a purifier; secondly. for puja (worship); thirdly, as the author has often seen it, to put a few drops in a glass of Persian sherbet offered to a friend or to a loved one. It is not only disposed off in the above ways, but it is also sold to those who are either too old or too poor to undertake a journey to fetch it for themselves. A great peculiarity of this water is that it never stagnates, but always keeps fresh, no matter for how long. Is this because it is mixed with the dust of the millions of the dead, whose grave yard this river is?

In the Central Provinces, third of Vaisakh is observed in a different manner. The day is reserved for doing something which is instrumental in giving shanti (peace) to the souls of parents who are dead. For this ceremony, the Brahmins are called in to be worshipped. One day before this day, an oral invitation to them is sent through one of the family; or the head of the family goes and extends it personally, and says that his meal will be served at a particular time. The ceremony of feeding is generally performed in the forenoon, and never after four o'clock in the afternoon. It should never be done in the dark. If both the father and the mother of the man are dead, he invites a Brahmin and his wife. If his mother only is dead, then he calls any old Brahmin woman for the meal—a young one, of course, will not come! If father is living, and mother and wife both are dead, then he generally calls one Brahmin woman for both of them, though two women are also called—one for mother and another for wife. The man is not supposed to do anything for his wife, as from a religious point of view the man's son is the only one who is really responsible for this. It is as a matter of courtesy that the husband calls in a Brahmin woman for her too. The Brahmin and his wife, when invited on this occasion, sit at meals together, contrary to the age-long convention of wife's taking her meals after the husband has finished.

The place where the Brahmin is asked to be seated is nicely plastered over with fine cow-dung mixed with a little earth, and it is printed over with various kinds of white designs made by filling a perforated tin plate with powdered chalk, and then gently striking it against the ground.

As soon as the Brahmin sits down, one red earthenware pitcher, in the name of the father, and one small 'gadwa' (an earthenware pitcherlike utensil —with a hole in the side) in the name of the mother are filled with fresh water and brought in. The hole in the side of the small 'gadwa' does not signify anything in particular, but is made as a matter of 'dastur' or custom.

The pitcher is kept on a big leaf or on many leaves of dhak (*Frondosa Bretea*) sewn together,— and on the top of it is kept the small 'gadwa'. On the leaf are placed all the different kinds of nice things made that morning; or rather, they are placed round the pitcher. The head of the family then proceeds with the regular worship of the earthenware and of the Brahmin. He throws some rice on the utensils, besmears them with red powder, throws flowers on them and marks them with sandalwood paste As he does this, he speaks to this effect: "I am doing this thing for the sake of my parents, for the peace and comfort of their souls, etc." After it he takes a little of each eatable that has been placed round the pitcher, puts it on the leaf, and makes it into a morsel which he gently sprinkles over the pitcher with the help of some mantras. He then takes a brass plate, which contains all the materials of worship and has in it also a receptacle of kneaded flour burning a cotton wick in clarified butter. He takes it up and waves it in front of the pitchers which are kept one over the other. He bows to them and to the Brahmin with folded hands.

This done, the host proceeds to make arrangements for the Brahmin's food; the Brahmin has come after having his bath at home and clad in a single piece cloth wrapped round his loins, the proper dress for taking his food. The host spreads a big leaf in front of the Brahmin, and on it he puts all the choicest things which the ladies of the house have been able to prepare. It may be mentioned that the members of the family do not taste anything until the Brahmin has partaken of it first as otherwise it would be considered as 'jhuta' (the remnant or the 'left over') and it would not be considered as the first offering. In fact, even the head of the family has to keep fast until the Brahmin has had his fill. The Brahmin is given water to drink out of the two pitchers which are (brand) new—Kora—and never used before. Lying in front of the Brahmin are things which are not only the results of labour of the whole morning but of days together. Men go beyond their means to have as many, and as nice things as possible; the sole object is to please the Brahmin; the more he is pleased the better for the souls of the departed. The feeding of the Brahmin is understood to be doing no good to him beyond pleasing him; but it is believed that more he likes the dish and the more he has, the more will the departed be satisfied. It will relieve the misery of the soul. As far as the belief in quantity is concerned it may be put down for the reader's benefit that there are a certain kind of Brahmins found in certain parts of India who may conveniently be termed as 'professional eaters'. If such a Brahmin is invited to a feast he after having his fill is pressed to eat more. He refuses to do so; but the host offers him one anna for each laddu (sweetmeat balls) eaten. After eating two or three he stops again. He is offered four annas a piece, then eight annas, one rupee, five rnpees, ten rupees a piece, ultimately one asharfi—one pound—for a piece! He has by this time probably finished off quite a large quantity of sweets, and not to speak of the handsome fee. Further, the feast may be brought to him and not he to the feast, for he is probably too fat, and too unwieldy to move about!

This, however, has been a digression. The Brahmin has in front of him sweets of many kinds, special dishes of diverse kinds, puris and kachauris, ghewars and pappers and what nots. The ladies have spent days in preparing these things, simply in the hope of pleasing their departed ones. After the Brahmin has finished his breakfast, he is offered a nice 'pan' wrapped in pure silver leaf, which he begins chewing at once and the man then garlands him, and marks him on his forehead with sandalwood paste: and marks stripes of mixed sandalwood and kasturi paste on his wrists for coolness, for fragrance and to please him generally. Then the ladies of the house who have stayed inside all the time sending out this and that, now come out and with folded hands bow before him and before the pitchers. He then rises up and blesses the family and says that he is well satisfied with the whole arrangement and that he has had his fill of things given him for the purpose of satisfying and pleasing the souls of the departed ones. 'What else do they want? Is not this all that they wanted?' He blesses them again and starts out. He is given money also, and in many cases the pitchers too; but if not they are used at home. The fruits of the season must be offered to please the dead. Melons, water-melons are the fruits most often seen at this ceremony, as they are generally found in the markets during these days. They are cut and placed on the top of the pitchers, either to be eaten after the meals, or carried away by the priest.

In one of the North-West Frontier towns, the author observed that all the worshippers came out of their houses and sat by the side of a small stream or a tiny canal, running in front of their houses. They had new small pitchers filled up with fresh water, covered up with hand-fans, on the top of which were seen melons cut into pieces. They were all sitting in a line, each worshipper having a Brahmin sitting by and reciting some mantras. Though in the Central Provinces the women were not conspicuous near the place of worship, there the women were observed to be taking part in the pujah itself.

In North-West India, on this day the Brahmin is given the hand-fan and the earthernwares, etc., but in the Central Provinces these things, except the pitchers, are not generally given this day. On the anniversary of the death-day of the deceased, the Brahmin of the family is called and given an umbrella, a suit of clothes, a pair of shoes, a fan or any other useful thing of the kind, and also the fruits of the season. Just as feeding of the Brahmin appeases the appetite and quenches the thirst of the departed one the giving of the above mentioned things benefits the deceased in his journey in heaven in a similar manner. Surely the deceased requires a new pair of shoes every now and then; for there are no cobblers in heaven if they require mending and an umbrella for the Sun in heaven, otherwise how tedious would the journey be!

Among Mahars, low caste Hindus, the Akshya Tritiya day is observed on the same principle, but in a different manner. They prepare nice dishes and keep them on big leaves. They all sit down on a specially plastered ground in the order of seniority, the senior one nearest the food and he being the head of the family, mixes all the things together. As no Brahmin acts as a priest for thom, they themselves perform all the necessary Pujah which is naturally greatly modified, and is simpler. When bowing and folding of hands, etc., is finished they all—both men and women (mark this distinctive feature here)—hold each other's hand in order to show that the relatives, one and all, are anxious to do something for the soul of the departed. After this the head of the family calls out to the crows, "caw, caw, caw," until a few crows turn up; and as you know, one has not long to wait for them. He then throws, or rather places, the mixed eatables on the roof, and allows the crows to eat them unmolested. It is believed that by feeding the crows the departed ones are gratified in the same manner as when Brahmins are fed; even apart from their being taken as substitutes for Brahmins, they are capable of transmitting that satisfaction independently. They are considered veritable messengers of the dead. When the food has been given out to the crows those who are 'left behind' speak a few messages for those who have gone before. It is not only the Mahars alone that feed the crows on this occasion, but some Brahmins also have been observed to do the same; so feeding the crows is not necessarily a substitute for feeding the Brahmins. Besides pappar and chichuni, the other dishes made are quite chatpatti —very appetising—consisting of savoury and acid things, pepper and other spices. When feeding the Brahmin, the main idea is to please him by offering him very tasty dishes; but among the Mahars the main idea is to prepare those eatables which were greatly relished by the deceased when alive. The author saw the country wine also being poured on the roof—sometimes mixed with food—simply because when he (or she) was living he used to drink, the underlined idea being to gratify the soul with the material comforts of this world.

Dogs are also fed, specially black ones. They, along with crows, are regarded as ones of the court of Yama, the God of Death.

In the case of the Mahars at least, the ceremony is not performed in a very serious manner. If the crows do not come at the man's call, the neighbours make some funny remarks,—"They (the crows) won't come as the wines are not offered first!" "They do not like your food; they will come to us!" "They will get 'Bital' * if they touch your food!" and so on; until the man begins to abuse the crows most profusely to the great amusement of the neighbours. But the performers themselves go through the ceremoney in a most light-hearted way. They give the impression that they have to perform a very pleasant ceremony.

---

* A temporary or permanent ostracism, revoked only by a heavy fine or grand feast, which is almost always beyond the capacity of the victim to pay.

VATA-SAVITRI.

THIS festival takes place in the month of Jesyeth. Vata means Banyan tree; and Savitri is the name of the girl connected with the story.

The origin of the story is not known nor even the author of it. The tradition is, that Raja Prikshitti, who reigned in Dehli—Hastnapur—in the remote past, heard of the story from Ganemaejaya, who in turn had been told it by his father Viyas. Now, Viyas was a very learned man, and was considered an authority on everything pertaining to religion. He was, moreover, the author of some of the Epics (Puranas).

The story runs as follows:—When the Kashatri King Ashyopati Raja (king of horses) realized that he was not going to be blessed with children, he went to Brahma, the Creator, with the request that a child might be born to him. Brahma directed him to go to his wife, who (he said) could grant the boon. His wife did grant the boon, and in course of time a daughter was born to him. The child was named after the name of Brahma's Queen, Savitri. After some years, when Savitri, the girl, grew up to the marriageable age, her father looked round for a suitable husband, but having failed to obtain one, he decided to send the bride round the world in order that she might select a bridegroom for herself. In due time she started, with processions of horses and palanquins, with a full retinue of officers, servants and soldiers. She came across many princes of ancient houses possessing wealth untold; but she could not see her way to accepting any. One day while still on her journey she passed through a thick jungle where she saw a beautiful young man, Satyawan by name, apparently a wood-cutter. She saw that the man was looking after his blind parents who were living in the forest. Greatly impressed as she was by his filial love and devotion, she decided there and then that she would marry him, and she did so.

Now Satyawan was originally a prince and heir to a throne which was no more his. It was on account of the blindness of the parents that their territory was invaded and annexed by a neighbouring king. They were turned out and were obliged to live in the forest where Satyawan, as a true son, looked after them day and night.

Narad,* the great devotee, was a mischievous fellow in the sense that he delighted in annoying,

*Narad was a great devotee of gods, and though he had a physical body, could go about like a spirit anywhere in the world. He could go even in zenana or harem but he was always a

and instigating quarrels among people by creating some trouble or other. He told Savitri that it was foreordained that Satyawan should die soon. On hearing this, she requested him to avert the fate but he would not listen. And in fact, it so happened after a short time that Satyawan while cutting wood fell down from a tree and breathed his last.

Yama, the God of Death, came and threw his noose on the neck of Satyawan in order to take his soul away. Savitri, being a very chaste girl, could see the invisible Yama. She requested him not to take his life away. But he would not pay any heed to her words. He took Satyawan's life and started; but she followed him. Yama, being a god, could go anywhere; but Savitri, being a human being, might not be expected to have the power to do so. But curiously enough, she did follow him, over dale and den, hills and mountains. Yama

---

Brahmacharya, who never married and never indulged in sexual intercourse. He may be recognized by his top-hair, which always stands erect, with the rest of the head clean cropped. He has a loin-cloth wrapped round his body, a garland of flowers round his neck, and is always with a 'sittar' in one hand and the 'chipliya' in the other. The sittar is a kind of guitar; and the chipliya is a sort of musical instrument, which consists of a pair of small wooden blocks, attached together by means of a tape or two, perhaps two inches in length. There is a ring fixed in one block to fit into the thumb, and a couple of rings on the other for the fingers, and thus the blocks are struck against each other, while held in the palm of the hand; while bunches of tiny brass bells are attached to the blocks.

Narad sang songs always in praise of Vishnu and could go in the presence of all the gods, even Krishna offered him a chair!

He is also called Brahmarishi—The Great Sage.

flew about in the clouds; but so did Savitri, as she had gained the power of flying because of her purity and chastity. Yama repeatedly told her not to follow him, saying that he was helpless in the matter, because he had received orders from above. But she would not listen to him, and still followed him wherever he went. When Yama saw that there was no way out he stopped and asked her if she wanted any boon except the restoration of life to Satyawan; if so, he would readily and gladly grant her. But Savitri insisted on her old demand. Later on, Yama, somehow or other, came to promise her to grant her three boons. These three boons did not include restoration of life to Satyawan; but were:—1. the restoration of eye-sight to the parents of Satyawan; 2. the restoration of their kingdom to them; 3. the birth of eight sons to Savitri. Now the third boon meant that Satyawan had necessarily to come to life, for the procreation of the sons. So it was by mistake that Yama granted the last boon, not realizing the consequences thereof. He was however so pleased with her fidelity, that he finally agreed to grant Satyawan's life.

Satyawan had fallen from a banyan tree; and this is the reason why women perform the worship at this tree.

This ceremony is gone through by married women only—mostly young wives. Men take no part in this service.

As for the detail of the worship, I will describe the ceremony as I saw it in the Central Provinces. This ceremony cannot be performed at home, as a Banyan tree is essential. I have heard people say that on Vata-Savitri day it must rain; and frequently, it does rain. But on the particular day on which I went to see the actual worship of the Banyan tree, it did not rain, though the day was cloudy. Without paying the least thought to the danger of their costly sarees and other dresses being soiled or spoiled, the women go out in the mud and slush, in pouring rain and blistering wind, in order to perform the worship.

On the Festival day, group after group of women may be seen passing down the road, wending their way to the temple; all carrying brass plates containing the materials of worship, consisting of some cotton thread, water in a special receptacle, rice, sandalwood paste, flowers, a capsicule of kneaded flour containing ghee and a cotton wick, sweets, and fruits of the season, wheat, cocoanut, betelnuts, dried dates, red powder, turmeric, etc.

While some walk down quietly, others have in front some sort of musical band playing Indian tunes. Many follow a couple of men playing tom-tom and a trumpet with a shrill sound. It is not unusual to see a solitary woman following either a few bandsmen, or possibly little old woman, weakly striking a tom-tom. It seems strange that such a noise should draw attention to one woman only, when the music leads one to expect to see a big procession of women,—young, fair, or dignified,—clad in bright and costly sarees, with flowers in their hair.

At the place where I watched the observance of the Festival, the temple is situated on the right bank of a small and narrow 'nullah', which is made pucca at this place by the temple-people, and is crossed by a small wooden bridge. The temple is thickly shaded by the trees surrounding it, and especially the huge Banyan tree. But the temple looks deserted this day; as all the Pujaris and Brahmins have crossed over to the other side, to earn the fees so graciously given by the young brides.

On reaching the tree, the trunk of which is some 50 feet in circumference at the base, one finds it surrounded by a number of Brahmins and the girls who have come for worship.

Each girl comes and sits down near a Brahmin, and waits till he has finished with her predecessor. She moves up near to the tree. on the base of which one will find all the material of worship left over by the previous worshippers. The girl has all her material ready; and the Brahmin opens his few musty and brownish papers (which look as if they had been saved from fire just in time to avert complete destruction), handwritten or printed with some verses in Sanskrit. He recites either orally or from those leaves, and as he does so, he keeps instructing the girl when to throw the water (the idea of which is, to give a bath to the gods, just as the Brahmins themselves bathe before taking meals, and also to wash the material of worship) or flowers (to beautify the place), or red powder, or to light the flour-made lamp burning the cotton wick in clarified butter, fruits, wheat, rice, turmeric, etc., etc. The woman makes a circle of water round the eatables and then both she and the Brahmin close their eyes, in order to let the gods have the food. They are not supposed to open their eyes when the gods are eating, as this might be instrumental in throwing the 'evil eye' on the food of the gods and thus enrage them. Similary, Brahmins take their meals in private, in order to escape the 'evil eye' of a greedy fellow The gods are supposed to be eating meals while the eyes of the worshippers are closed. As a rule, this ceremony should take place at 12 o'clock; but I did not notice any strict observance of the time. After this, both the worshippers rise and offer a prayer. The woman bows to the priest, and to the tree three times, pays him a few pice and some fruits, encircles the tree with the cotton thread, going round it 7 times, and marks the tree with sandalwood paste, the fragrance of which is supposed to cheer the souls of the gods This done, she goes to her friends standing by, and wishes them, one by one, some good wish for herself, and incidentally for her husband also, and marks them with red powder in the forehead right above the nose. She is also herself marked in the same manner by them with the same kind of wish. Then any fruits which were left over are presented and exchanged, and before she departs, she distributes the rest to the sweepers and beggars who are waiting near by with their baskets, ready to receive them. This done she departs. This puja is conducted in a solemn manner; there is no noise, no confusion at the tree. Everything is quiet, except the murmuring of the priest, low voices of the girls, and the swish of the sarees. But at a distance, the harsh voice of the sweepers and beggars quarrelling over the eatables, might be heard. There was a marked and conspicuous absence of men near the trees, except for the Brahmins and myself. As for me, I was all the time nervous lest some graceful lady should approach me with fruits, taking me to be some "beggar" waiting for them! And I had the feeling of one who was knowingly treading on hallowed ground.

The ladies return to their homes in the same manner as they came, that is, with music, etc.; and with an air of satisfaction in their eyes.

At four in the afternoon, the ladies again gather together, this time in a house; and a matron who is expected to be well acquainted with the story of Savitri recites it in a sing-song manner. This is highly appreciated and patiently listened to. I once heard a good old lady reciting it whose voice was a little hoarse, and her laughter sounded like the flapping of a raven's wings; but she put life into the whole thing. Her voice would rise alternately in cadence of sorrow and of joy, of pity and astonishment. The women sat round with babies in their laps. The women have to keep fast from 6 a.m. to 6 a.m. of the next day; but their fast is not as strict as that of the Mohammedans; for they are allowed to take fruits and milk, but not grains or things which contain grains.

THE ECLIPSE

LONG ago, when the gods in their search for a means of attaining immortality churned the ocean, they procured Nectar or Amrit. And at a reception, when all were busy drinking it and making merry, a demon, by name Rahu, quietly crept in and took up a bowl to drink it. The sacred liquid had hardly gone down his throat when the sun and the moon noticed it and reported the matter to Vishnu who immediately severed the demon's neck from his body by throwing his discus at the thief, and also cut off both his arms. No sooner was the body rent in twain than the head and the tail flew apart and got fixed in the sky as two planets, by name Rahu and Ketu; and in order to wreak vengeance they still keep running after the sun and the moon. And they have their revenge at least twice a year, once on the sun and once on the moon. Some say that as the head still had some nectar, it became immortal, and though the body died, the head has not yet forgotten its injury. It is also said by some that it actually swallows them, others say that it throws its shadow on them in its effort to swallow them. The name of the demon of eclipse—Rahu—signifies "seizer" or "looser". This irate demon Rahu, a great mischief-maker, had four arms and his lower part tapered in a tail and is often represented as a black man riding on a lion.

It is believed that by taking a bath in a sacred river the demon is scared away and the release of the afflicted sun or the moon is hastened. Such is the idea of many a Hindu who takes a ceremonial bath on this occasion. The scene of countless thousands of people bathing at this time is most impressive in places like Calcutta, Bombay, Allahabad or Benares. No sooner is the sun or the moon seen in the grip of Rahu than the din is turned into an impressive hush and silence, and then the cries of 'Chhor do, Chhor do' (leave it, leave it) begin. The full significance of the scene can be well comprehended by a Hindu alone. Men, women and children come from long distances and suffer great privations; yet they remain undaunted and return to their homes after they have washed their sins in the sacred rivers and thus begin life anew. And so from year to year the sins are washed off and carried away to the sea.

In Calcutta, the banks of the Hooghly and the Ghats are full of humanity on these occasions. When the eclipse begins after a short hush, the cymbals clang, the bells peal, the gongs go, the shells blow and the noise does not sound as if of this world, but it is like the fall of a far-off river. In Bombay, the people generally go to Chowpatti to bathe in the sea. Some rub their body with Til seeds, as these seeds are considered acceptable to the sun; as, on January 14th of 1926, the festival of Til Sankrant fell on the same day, it doubled the value of the day as well as the bath. On the same day on the holy Ganges at Allahabad two million five hundred thousand Hindus bathed; the reason of this mighty concourse being the coincidence of Amavasya—the completely moonless dark night, Til Sankrant and the eclipse of the sun, all falling on the same day. An eclipse is always an auspicious occasion for bathing in the Ganges and then it was doubly so, also because the 14th of January 1926 (Thursday) was the last day of the month of Paus; on this day every Hindu is anxious to take a bath. The eclipse on this day coincided with the entry of the sun into the asterism of "Makar" which corresponds to Capricorn. The sun was on the most southerly point of the Zodiac. A Hindu year from this day is divided into two. The first six months are considered 'lucky', in the sense that those Hindus who die during that period go straight off to heaven, while those who expire in the other half have to wait in a sort of waiting-hall till the gates of heavens open again when the first day of the lucky six months arrives.

It is considered very auspicious for a solar eclipse to fall on a Sunday and a lunar eclipse to take place on a Monday. If it does so, it is called

Chudamani—a jewel with a crestlike appearance or a jewel like the comb of a cock.

It is not necessary for people to go to particular places for their bath. If there is no place of pilgrimage or a sacred river or a lake near by, they can go to a well or a tank or bathe at home.

In Maharashtra, the bath is taken immediately after the eclipse is seen. There should not be any delay in the matter. After this bath one should take a rosary and with the same wet cloth on in which the bath was taken, should sit down and spend the whole dark period in prayer and meditation. As soon as the eclipse is over the devotee should have another dip and wash himself clean. In the places of pilgrimage situated on the banks of the rivers which are considered sacred, it is a great sight to see hundreds of men and women bathing at one time, raising their hands in awe and reverence.

Moreover it is held that everyone is unclean during an eclipse, and should bathe and wash away that uncleanliness. Rahu renders even the gods unclean. Similarly there are other things also which are defiled by an eclipse. Tradition says that even the old clothes, not only those worn at the time of the eclipse, but also all clothes in the house, should be given away in charity though people do not do this except in the case of really old clothes. Other things which are defiled because of the eclipse are the cooked food which should not be eaten but given away to the poor; water that has lain in the house during that period should be thrown away and even the earthen pots used for holding water should be broken. During an eclipse all household business is suspended. A Hindu will not touch his food nor drink water, and for fear of demons he will not sleep during this period, but he will repeat the Gayatri Mantras against all pollution and defilement. The sun and the moon themselves are polluted and they pollute everything on which their light falls. Pregnant women are not allowed to see an eclipse nor are they allowed to thread a needle, for that matter they are not allowed even to see a needle, for if they do so, their children will be born crippled or one-eyed or blind. Nobody is allowed to sleep during an eclipse lest demons should attack him unaware. No marriage takes place during this period. Nothing new is started till after it. In the case of lunar eclipse one must fast for three hours before the time, and for nine hours before in the case of solar eclipse.

Those who are considered masters in the art of curing minor ailments by chanting mantras and by blowing breath on the affected parts, use the period of eclipse for obtaining further hold on such powers; especially those who know how to cure wasp-sting, scorpion-sting, snake bite and those who are under the influence of demons, witches and ghosts. They go as far as possible into the middle of the river, stream or tank—generally waist-deep—and there repeat the mantras which were taught them by their gurus. A guru who promised to initiate the author into the mysteries of curing snake-bite had made it a condition that the ceremony was to take place in the middle of a stream. When thousands are bathing on the river banks, a number of such men can be seen in the middle of the stream chanting mantras with claspsed hands.

It may be mentioned that any Hindu who is born in the constellation in which an eclipse takes place has to perform extra-ceremonies in order to make himself immune against any misfortune that may befall him as a result of such coincidence; for it is very inauspicious for the time to have to belong to such a constellation.

In big places like Calcutta and Bombay, the beggars reap a big harvest at the time of an eclipse, which may even be considered a festival of the beggars! On this occasion a Hindu is enjoined to give in charity grains, old clothes, eatables, money, etc., and the beggars know this; so they come out of their hiding places, ill-clad, wretched-looking, miserable, dirty and full of sores—a whole army of them; and they squat on the roadsides and clamour for alms, even at times snatching alms. After passing through companies of these struggling and noisy beggars, raising clouds of dust through the heat of their activity, one emerges more like a beggar oneself than a devotee going to, or coming from, a bathing-ghat! In North India, the sweepers are the people who are entitled to beg and receive alms. Although, through an agreement among themselves, they are expected to beg from the people in their respective Mohallas—localities in which they work—yet they do encroach on each other's territory; and not only that, each member of his or her family goes out with a basket and brings it full of grain or other things. In a lunar eclipse they flit about like ghosts with soft thud of their bare feet. They go in and out of winding lanes in feverish activity, calling at each house, saying "De dan Chhute Grahn"—(Give alms and the eclipse will be over) the reason why this is said is that by charity God is pleased and in return He will save the sun or the moon from the clutches of Rahu. The devotees try to rescue the sun and the moon from their great affiiction. Many a sweeper and a beggar has been disappointed at the door of the author on occasions of eclipse, considering him an ungodly Hindu! The author has thus watched them year after year hurrying ahout in the subdued light of the moon and crossing each other after the manner of warp and woof. It is a weird scene.

In the Centrel Provinces, though any beggar might go and beg, it is only the Mangs—professional musicians employed for ceremonial occasions, and one of the lowest castes,—who have a traditional right to beg on such an occasion. They go to the houses of their patrons and others, and get old clothes, grains, money and such other things as are to be disposed of by the Hindus.

Though some see a solar eclipse through a dark glass, others take a shallow copper plate or basin and pour some water in it and then take a *moosal* (pestle) of wood (generally used for pounding rice) which is held erect in the basin. This pounder is about 2½ feet long and is round, with a diameter of about four to five inches and both the ends are so rounded off that it cannot stand on its ends and impossible to make it stand on a flat surface. This pestle is held straight in the middle of the flat basin containing water. It is placed there a little before the time the eclipse is due. As soon as the eclipse has begun, the hand is taken off the pestle which stands by itself and does not fall until the eclipse is over. So this is one way in which people are able to know the exact time of the beginning and the end of an eclipse which in the case of the sun—when it is a partial eclipse—they might not be able to see on account of the dazzling light.

VYAS PUJA

(Guru Puja)

ON the full moon day of the month of Asadha worship is offered to Vyas, the sage who is credited with having written the great Vedas of the Hindus. He must have been truly a great man; and he is considered a great Guru.

Vyas Puja is now-a-days taken to mean 'Guru Puja'—the worshipping of one's own religious teacher or guru. In the days gone by, every Hindu used to have his own guru, and even now there are quite a number who do so, especially those who have not yet been affected by the rising tide of modern civilization. Naturally therefore, only those observe this Guru Puja who have gurus; and such gurus are given the status of gods, and are actually worshipped as such. After the ground has been nicely plastered, the guru is asked to sit there, with only his loin-cloth on, and his legs crosswise. A Brahmin priest is called in, who recites suitable mantras for the occasion, and proceeds to instruct the student to throw certain material of worship on the head of the guru, exactly as it is done in the case of the worship of a god. The priest asks him to throw flowers and coloured rice on the guru's head, and put a garland of flowers round his neck, and then to put a mark of sandalwood paste on his forehead, with a few grains stuck on to it. After the worship is over, the guru is given nice things to eat, which are specially prepared for the occasion. After finishing his meal, the guru blesses the student, who touches the feet of the guru with either his hands or forehead, and then waits upon him at a respectful distance with clasped hands.

In these days, by gurus are meant not only those people who teach the Vedas or give religious instruction of any kind, but also those who teach their chelas (disciples) certain mantras to control evil spirits, or to cure snake-bite, scorpion-sting, etc. Such gurus are generally held in great awe by their disciples.

EKADASI

AS the name suggests, this festival falls on the eleventh day of the lunar month. There are 24 Ekadasis in a year, one falling every fortnight, regardless of whether it falls during the dark or the light fortnight. Hindus are very particular to observe this day; as the merit gained by observing even one such day properly is believed to be equal to the devoting of sixty thousand years of worship and prayer; so this obviously offers an astonishingly short cut to Mukti or salvation, for which one chance is given every fortnight! All that the worshippers have to do, is to observe a fast, and keep themselves busy the whole day in religious thought and meditation, or reading holy books. In a Hindu fast, one can eat fruits or drink milk, but one should not take anything made of grain. Some people do not take anything, not even water; this is called Nirjali (waterless) Ekadasi; while in the case of those who take water only and nothing else, it is called Karak Ekadasi. The worshipper has to have his bath early in the morning, and recite mantras; on his way back from the well or stream he should not look about him as he might inadvertently see something which is not pure or holy; for example, a man of low caste, or a wicked man; and he should try to close his ears also, in order not to hear anything unworthy. In short, he has to keep away on this day from all that is low or impure, or likely to turn his thoughts away from things which are worthy and noble. It is not very clear why people resort to places of pilgrimage, when by observing just one day in this way, they can attain all that they desire. But the observance of Ekadasi is enjoined in the Puranas; and from boyhood onward every Hindu is expected to observe it. There are many who are careless or unable to keep this day every fortnight, but there are two special Ekadasis in a year which must be observed at any cost. These are called Maha-Ekadasis—the Great Ekadasis. Before proceeding further, it may be mentioned that these Ekadasis are observed by the followers of the God Vishnu, and the observance of these Ekadasi days has been inaugurated comparatively recently, so that they might correspond to the fast-days of the followers of Shiva. In the Central Provinces, the followers of both gods observe these days.

The legend of their origin is as follows:—Mridumanya, a demon, was such a faithful devotee of Shiva, that the god promised him immortality, so that no human being, not even a god, would be able to kill him. Only a woman could kill him, and one who herself had not been born of woman.

When the gods found that the demon was getting on their nerves', and was no longer tolerable, they went and waited on the three Great Gods—Shiva, Vishnu and Brahma—to save them from the demon. So the 'Big Three' went to a mountain, and entered a cave, with the purpose of keeping a fast and disentangling Shiva from the promise he had made to the demon. Now in this cave, when rain was falling, they sat so closely huddled together, that out of their breath, which was thicker than fog, there was produced a woman, who not being born of a man, was able to kill the demon in a fight. The name of that woman was Ekadasi; and she killed the demon on the eleventh day. Now anyone—as advised by Ekadasi —who has a bath (as the Gods took an involuntary bath on account of the rain!) and keeps a fast on the eleventh day of every lunar fortnight, will be able to overcome sin and evil. There are other reasons also why Ekadasi is held sacred by Hindus. Some say that the spirit of Ekadasi came out of the body of Krishna himself on the eleventh day of the light half of the month of Mangsar or Margasirsha. Another reason is, that Nammalvar, one of the greatest saints of the Vaishnavas, attained salvation on this day in the presence of the thirty-three crores (330 millions) of gods.

The two Maha Ekadasis, as stated above, are observed in connection with the God Vishnu's sleep in the light half of the month of Asadh, and his waking on the eleventh day of the light half of the month of Kartikka. In the light half of Asadh, this Ekadasi is observed as usual with prayer and fasting. As the result of Vishnu's keeping fast, on this day rain fell after three years' drought on this earth; and people observe it in memory of this event, though there are hardly any who think of this legend. On this day the worshippers of the God Vishnu put his image in a sleeping posture, lying on one side, to show that the god has resorted to the depth of the ocean, to snatch his four months' sleep. He finishes his sleep on the eleventh day of the light half of the month of Kartikka, which is also the day of Tulsi Marriage, and the last day of the rains. People may now go out for picnics or excursions without much fear of being drenched. The image of Vishnu is then made to sit up to show he has wakened from his sleep.

Thousands of people go annually at the Maha Ekadasi Festivals to Pandharpur, a place of pilgrimage in the Bombay Presidency, to worship in the temple of Pandarnath, an incarnation of Vishnu, —though he is not one of the 10 famous incarnations of Vishnu, of which 9 have already appeared, and the tenth will come some time towards the end of this world. This pilgrimage is held on both the Maha Ekadasi days. It is chiefly the Vaishnavites who go to this place, though the Saivites also come. The difference between the Saivites and the Vaishnavites in the northern as well as the central parts of India is so little that no cleavage exists between the two communities; but this cleavage is strongly apparent in South India. By some people it is believed that Pandarnath, whose other names are Vithoba, or Vithal, or Pandurang, was also an incarnation of Buddha.

Pundalik was the the first devotee of Pandarnath, and it was for him that Vishnu became incarnate. Other devotees of his were Dnayan Deo and Tukaram. These two men were great writers and poets. Dnayan Deo was a great preacher also, and it was he who interpreted into Mahrathi language the religious knowledge of the Hindus given in Sanskrit; so he is considered to have laid the foundation of Hindu worship in the Maharashtra. And what was left by him was completed by Tukaram. The names of other devotees of Pandarnath are, Damaji, a Brahmin; Chokhamela, an untouchable Mahar, and the only saint of the Mahar, born 540 years ago; Goroba, a potter; Narsingwa Mehta, a Brahmin; Neurati Dnayan Deo, the younger brother of Dnayan Deo, Sopan, another brother of Dnayan Deo, and their sister Mukta Bai; Namdeo, a tailor; and Janabai, a domestic servant of Namdeo.

The story of Pundalik is interesting. As a boy he was disobedient to his parents and did not care for them. As he grew up, he became a profligate, and spent his money on prostitutes and in gambling.

He was so fond of women that he did not for one moment even like to part with them, so wherever he went he would carry his wife or a woman on his shoulder. A day came when he began beating his parents, and after a while turned them out to wander alone in the world. He himself did not thrive for long, as he became poor and had to go about begging, till one day a saintly man, a guru, by name Kukut Swami, saw him in this bad condition. As he noticed Puddalik's bad state, he took him into a thick jungle where he showed him wild animals, tigers and wolves, and black cobras attacking him. Pundalik was so frightened that he fell down at the feet of Kukut Swami, and asked him to command him to do whatever he liked. Kukut Swami was himself a devoted son of his parents. He had devoted his whole life in the Seva or service of his parents, and he told Pundalik to do the same, saying that this was one way of attaining the bliss of salvation. Thereupon Pundalik began to search for his old parents, and on finding them he began serving them with all devotion and sincerity. He served them so well that the god Vishnu himself once came down to 'have his Darshan', *i.e.*, to see him. At that time Pundalik was so busy serving his parents that he did not so much as turn and see who the outsider was; but instead, he picked up a brick, and flung it in his direction, telling the visitor to stand upon it and wait till he had finished serving his parents. When he had finished his filial duty, he turned towards the god, who was so pleased with his devotion to his parents, that he immediately took him up to heaven in his 'Udan Khatola'—a kind of aeroplane! Pundalik certainly did not forget his parents, for he took them along also to heaven, where doubtless they are enjoying eternal life!

Kukut Swami's purpose in looking after Pundalik was to save him from a life of misery by becoming his guru, and by asking him to devote his life to the service of his own parents. According to a legend, the rivers Ganges, Jamuna, Godavari, Krishna, Kaveri and Pannar used to come to the house of Kukut Swami every morning, in order to do his ordinary household work such as cooking, scouring of utensils and sweeping of the house; and before leaving his house they used to 'see his face' in order to get their own sins of the previous day and night whitewashed. But once when they saw the face of Pundalik—who by the way lived in the house of his gurn for some time—their own faces were immediately turned black because Pundalik was such a great sinner; and they were turned fair again, only when Kukut Swami threw the resplendence of his own face on them. So great was the sinfulness of Pundalik. In the temple of Pandharpur, you may see standing face to face, the Pundalik and the Incarnation of Vishnu *i.e.*, Vithal and his wife.

NAG PANCHMI

THE word 'Nag' means 'cobra', and 'Panchmi' means 5th. This festival of the Cobra is called Nag Panchmi, because it falls on the 5th of the month of Sravan. Though the cobra is the proper kind of snake for worship, yet any kind of snake will do. The origin of this festival is traced through customs imported from foreign countries; but it has authority in the Vedas, where it is enjoined that the snake should not only go about unmolested, but should also be fed with milk and worshipped in all awe. Among Hindus there is great confusion of thought about this snake-worship, as all sorts of legends are recounted in order to give reasons for the inclusion of snake-worship in the list of religious customs. From North to South and from West to East, one comes across different ceremonies and customs, but with the same end in view.

The following are a few of these legends and ceremonies, which will at least serve to give the reader an idea of the significance of snake-worship:—

1. A great and powerful but mischievous Rakshas (demon) by name Shankasur, once pushed

the Earth to Patal, the nether-world and disappeared. When the gods and the other Rakshasas saw what had happened, they at once set to thinking as to the best method of bringing it up. They took the huge mountain Meru, and placed it erect in the ocean, with one end on the bottom and the other end above the surface of the water. As they could not get a big rope to wrap round it, they requisitioned instead the services of a huge Nag (snake), Vasuki by name, for the purpose of churning the ocean, in order that the Earth might come up to the surface, just as butter comes up after a little churning of milk. However, the gods got hold of the serpent's tail, and the Rakshasas of his head, and they began churning the ocean with tremendous force and power, until the great disturbance produced, as it were, the Earth from the womb of the sea. Imagine the confusion !— the terrifying noise of the gurgling of the water which seemed as if it would rend the very skies. However, in due time, not only the earth, but nine 'ratans' (gems) also came out ; *viz.*,—Hira (diamond), Manak, Moti (pearl), Nilum (the precious blue stone), Spthik, Pola (a stone of red colour), Turmari, Lasniya, and Pushparaja. Apparently, the precious stones named above appeared in this world for the first time on that occasion. Along with the nine 'ratans' there came up to the surface the following also: Laxmi, who was immediately appropriated by Vishnu as his wife, a big Sankh (conch shell), an

Aeravata (an elephant with ten trunks), Ashva (horse), Amrut (the water of life which must have been drunk by the gods by mistake!), Vish (poison), the Sun and the Moon. This looks like the beginning of the creation of our world! Now all the 'ratans' and other things that came out of the ocean were divided among the gods; but no one was willing to take Vish (poison). Immortal Shiva relieved the others of the difficulty by voluntarily drinking it. No sooner had he done it than his body began to burn like fire, through its effect. Feeling helpless, and looking for coolness, he kept the moon on his head to serve as an ice bag and specially called the river Ganges to fall on his head ; but all to no effect. He looked round and caught hold of a huge cobra and wrapped it round his neck to impart coolness to the throat, but this too, though it helped a little, did not make any appreciable difference. (It is said that the lower part of a snake is very cold!) As a last resort, he began reciting Rama's name which had immediate effect and relieved him of his suffering. Now it is asserted that people have begun worshipping the snake, because the gods used it as a rope for churning the ocean, and because Shiva was benefited by it to a certain extent.

2. The second legand is that the Earth is supported on the head of a huge snake called Shesha, though a special seat is reserved on its head for Vishnu also. The Earth is not resting on any solid

thing but on the surface of water. This should give no reason for worship, unless it compels insignificant human beings to do so through the awe it inspires. It is the same kind of legend as the one that says that the Earth is supported on the horns of a cow; earthquakes being considered as nothing but the shaking of the Earth when it is shifted from one horn to the other, when the cow is tired.

3. Another story is that a certain girl, no longer able to bear the indifference of her husband and the taunts and corporal punishment of her mother-in-law, fled to the jungle, where she was taken care of by a cobra; who being greatly pleased with her told her the great secret that whosoever worshipped him would be saved from the dangers and calamities of this world. This news was apparently conveyed to the people, who experimented and found it correct; and so this secret is now known to everyone!

4. Another legend says that Krishna and Kaliya (a huge water-snake) had a fight in the Jamna river. Krishna, after having defeated Kaliya, brought him over to Gokul, where the Gopis—the 16,000 milk-maid playmates of Krishna—constantly fed him with milk.

In North India, a festival corresponding to Nag Panchmi is observed in the month of Asarh and not in Sravan. It is held that Mansa, the mother-snake, protects people from all harm during the four rainy months when Vishnu is having his nap in the nether-world. In the Central Provinces this deity is unknown, nor do people observe any such day on this date.

Now, it has been observed that the worship is conducted differently in different places, though the object in view is the same. Women make figures of a snake with chalk or sandalwood paste on doors or walls and worship it. Some make a model of a snake out of cow-dung, which is thrown away on the next day of the worship; and those who can afford to do so, such as Rajas and Zamindars, make ones of silver and gold. Worship is conducted with the help of Brahmins, husband and wife worshipping either together or separately. The materials of worship are:—sandalwood paste, wood apple (bel) leaves, flowers, coloured rice, red powder, camphor, a lamp burning cotton wick in clarified butter, garlands of flowers and turmeric. Milk is very necessary, and is kept in front of the image or the drawing, and the snake is supposed to drink it—but it is the cat which generally enjoys it! If one comes across a live snake that day, every effort is made to make him drink the milk. Snake-charmers generally earn a lot on this day; for they go about from house to house showing Cobras, Pythons and other kinds of snakes and getting in return money, clothes and milk. Women most reverently bow before them with clasped hands. The materials of worship described above are thrown round the image under the instructions of the priest.

Indian corn or maize is another thing which is generally used in this worship. One way is to fill a brass vessel with it and keep it along with the milk in front of the image; the other is to go to a white-ant-mound in the jungle (after the worship of the snake-image is done at home) and keep a vessel full of milk near by and a quantity of maize parched in hot sand near it. Such ant-mounds are considered to be the abodes of cobras, because they generally do not like to leave such a comfortable abode if they once find one. Worship at the ant-mound is usually resorted to, only in case there is no public snake 'temple' or cell. But such 'temples' are found in India in millions. Every basti-settlement, every village has its own stone snake-image, made at the head of a platform and covered with a toy-house. The rich have their own silver and gold images, which are kept either in the worship-room of the house or in the sitting room, where they are worshipped daily.

If a Nag is killed by mistake, an image of it is made and kept for worship. The author saw such a memorial to a snake the other day, a big brick platform with a snake image at the top of it. Here a cobra was killed by mistake, and was burnt and buried on the spot.

Hindus do not kill snakes, and if ever they come across one, are careful to try to catch it alive and to take to a distant place to be let loose. It is quite interesting to watch the way they catch a snake for removal to the jungle near by. A few months back, the author had not only the opportunity of seeing a snake being captured, but also the way in which milk was first offered to it to drink. The old woman in whose house the snake was found came out shouting excitedly, "Snake! snake!" A few men ran towards her house to find a bluish sort of snake quietly lying on the clean mud floor beside the hearth. The woman first insisted on giving it some milk which she did in a brass saucer but he declined to accept it. After she had clasped her hands and bowed to it she requested the men to remove it. The author was a bit surprised to see a pair of ordinary small tongs being employed in trying to catch the snake which was some twenty-eight inches in length. After chasing it round, in and out the eathenware pots kept in the corner, it was ultimately driven towards the mouth of a pot touching the ground. No sooner had it gone in than a piece of cloth was tied on the top and carried some two furlongs outside the town, and let loose!

On Nag Panchmi Day, special things are cooked especially things which have been cooked on such occasions in the family from the very beginning—eatables which have become a tradition in the family. Some, for instance, make 'Puran Puri' on this day, because their forefathers have been always making this special thing on this day. This special preparation—sweet biscuits dipped into hot ghee or milk—is generally eaten by most Hindus of the Central Provinces. This is not the only kind of dish eaten; the idea is to maintain and to carry on the tradition of eating a particular thing on this day. But it is considered perfectly legitimate, if long before this day a vow were seriously taken to do a particular thing in opposition to the tradition of the family. Some take a vow that on Nag Panchmi Day they will keep a fast, others that they will eat such and such nice things, even though in the family the tradition has been just the opposite. It must be trying for families having a common courtyard, that some should fast and others feast! Nag Panchmi is 'a day of traditions'. All sorts of traditions are maintained, some of them funny and amusing. Some families have a tradition not to get up from sleep on the Nag Panchmi morning, unless told to do so by a member of another family. Even if they are awake they have to pretend to be fast asleep. Now it sometimes happens that for the sake of enjoying the fun, the persons who were requested the previous night to wake them up do not do so for some hours; so that people crowd round their beds, talking, shouting, and jokingly saying funny things to the sleepers, who of course are so 'fast asleep that they cannot hear all that is being said round them! Perhaps at last an elderly man, of a religious type, unable to bear any longer the insults meted out to the sleepers, goes finally and tells them to get up; or if things have gone too far and the rouser does not keep his word, the sleeping woman, unable to stand it any longer just raises her head for a moment and curses, for awakening her, the man who ought to have roused her and then at once closes her eyes in sleep again. Then probably the man, now realizing that the limit has been reached, goes forward and formally tells her to get up. Then the cursing and shouting of the women of the family bring forth another festival!

As observed above, the Hindu people are very careful not to kill a snake, especially on this day; and if one is killed it is burnt and buried on the spot, and a pucca platform made on it, with an image on the head of it. If, on the other hand, a man is bitten and dies this day, Nag Panchmi is never again observed by the family, this disregard being a sort of punishment to the snake-god or gods; for surely a general immunity should be declared by them at least for this day! But this is true in the case of other festivals also. If a death takes place on any of the festivals, that festival is never observed again by the family; unless a birth takes place on the same festival in the future, which would mean that the life which had been taken away by the gods was returned in the shape of a baby. But how remote are the chances of a death and a birth taking place on the same festival day. In order, therefore, not to kill accidentally a snake or any creeping thing of that shape, people do not do much of cooking that day, and they are forbidden to use a 'tawa' (iron plate used for making chappaties) on this festival.

We may record here the manner in which the Mahars—the low caste Hindus—generally observe this festival. In a Mahar Basti or settlement, the people rise early, and take a bath; and especially in the brotherhood of those Mahars who by means of mantras cure snake-bitten victims, they go round and collect a little money from the basti, and go to the bazaar and purchase the following things for the worship:—cocoanuts, 'ud batti' (a kind of incense), Gulal (pink powder), camphor, murmure (parched rice) or Lai (millet), garlands, leaves of the wood-apple tree, milk, dates, almonds, leaves of nim tree (melia), a little cotton containing a few drops of scent, and two biras of pan—(each bira made of five leaves) one bira for the monkey god and the other for the ant-hill worship, and containing nuts, laung, Jaitri, and Jaïfail, and also Pachkhaja which is a special preparation of five ingredients used for worship. Madrasis living in the Central Provinces include an egg also, besides many of the above things. They arrange all these things in a big tray and keep them on the roadside, where the brotherhood gathers together to start on a procession to the stream, on the bank of which is situated a tiny temple of Maruti, the monkey-god. The procession forms into two groups, one in front of the other, with the tray in the middle. The two groups as they start for the stream sing *'bari'* turn by turn, so pathetically that many begin to weep.

The *Bari* consists of two parts; the first having verses in flattering praise of the Cobra, such as were once recited to me by the son of the leading Dhantari, "O Great Cobra, thy eyes are like the red rubies, and thy ears like the Chaj* and thy tongue is as fine as a needle, etc.. etc." and requesting also that he should have mercy on mankind and desist from biting them. The second part is a fervent prayer to the first *Dhantari* (the *guru* who first taught mankind how to counteract Cobra-poison) asking him to destroy the Cobra who is the enemy of mankind. They sing his praises also.

When the cobras, who are expected to be within hearing distance of the doleful ditty, hear men singing in their praise, they lift up their heads and expand their hoods and sway right and left in great exultation. The other part of the song, consisting

---

* A flat tray-like thing of straw used by women for cleaning rice and grain by shaking it right and left, and then giving it an upward jerk which process separates husks and stones from the grains—winnowing basket.

of a request to the first Dhantari to destroy cobras, is not supposed to be heard by them! The idea is to persuade the cobras to desist from their dreadful activities or to lessen them at least, and on the other side get old Dhantari busy in their destruction!

Thus turn by turn they go on singing, and reach the stream and the temple of Maruti, where the god is worshipped with the material in the tray; the cocoanuts are broken there and collected. The Mahars cannot get Brahmins to guide them in worship. From there they start again and begin singing the same thing over again until they reach a 'Dhombar'—an ant-hill which is considered to be an abode of big cobras. The ant-hill which the author saw was situated in a place surrounded by bungalows of rich Hindus, and no one dare erect a bungalow in the vacant ground in which the ant-hill is situated. After worshipping it in the same manner as at the temple of Maruti, they leave milk for the cobra to drink, and go back to the place on the road from where they had started. Here the broken pieces of cocoanuts, considered as a kind of sacrament, are distributed among the women and children of the Basti. Soon after, those people, especially the curers of snake-bites, go to their houses and do the same worship with the same sort of material there also, but with the addition of the following:—In one corner of the teapoy on which other things of worship are placed, there are arranged in three parallel rows, five scorpions, five cobras and five lamps, all made of kneaded flour ;—the scorpions nearest the worshipper, the cobras in the middle and the Divas (lamps—burning wicks of rolled up cotton in clarified butter held in a flour-capsule) the farthest away. Then ordinary worship is gone through with incense. The scorpions, the cobra (of three to four inches in length) and Divas are made in a peculiar way. They are shaped and placed in an earthenware or iron cooking pot containing a little water, the surface of which should have been previously covered over with a layer of broken wicker, or the thick straw of which the native brooms are made, and on top are spread Dhak leaves (*Frondosa Bretea*). The degchi should be covered and fire lit under it. The scorpions, the cobras and the lamps should be taken out when sufficiently steamed. After worship these things should be eaten by dipping them in ghee or milk, and the full meal, if required, should be taken after it.

In order not to kill inadvertently a cobra, or a creeper of its shape of howsoever small a size no hand mill is used for grinding grain that day, nor anything like spices ground on a stone slab lest there be any cobra which may have come in in the shape of a small worm! The story which will follow later on will show how a great Rajah was bitten by a huge cobra which had taken the form of a worm in a plum. People actually go to the length of avoiding anything which bears resemblance to a snake in any way; for example, *Sev*, a spicy preparation made of flour which being thin like string become crooked and zigzag like snakes when fried in oil or ghee. There are two or three kinds of vegetables which in shape and size grow like snakes, are never eaten by such people. Europeans, for example, would not eat vermicelli that day if they were Mahars.

The following is the legend of the first Dhantari:

It was decreed by tho gods that the great Rajah Priksheti should die of the bite of Taksaka the Cobra on a fixed day. The Rajah, in order to take every precaution, built himself such a novel and fine cage of steel that even if a fly sat on it, it would be cut into two by the sharp edges of the outer frame of the cage. Physicians, Doctors, and others who claimed to save the Rajah from the snake came from all parts of the world, for he had advertised that he would give away half of his kingdom and his wealth to any one who would save him. One man by name Dhantari who when he heard this news, spoke to his wife and said, "Wo are poor and have nothing for our old age. Let me go and try to save the Rajah and get the wealth in order to enable us to live in comfort for the rest of our life." Now Taksaka tho Cobra had probably tested tho doctors that they could not save tho Rajah, so he wanted to be sure about Dhantari also. Taksaka turned himself into a Brahmin and came on Dhantari's way and asked him whither he was bound. On getting the proper answer, the snake declared that he could not really cure a snake-bite and immediately he turned himself into a snake again and wrapped himself round a big tree which he bit. The tree at once became dry and almost like ashes. By force of his mantras Dhantari brought the tree again to its original freshness. Now Taksaka found that he had to cope with a powerful adversary. Finding that Dhantari being a poor man wanted wealth and had no further interest in the affair, he offered him fifty potfuls of gold, with permission to carry home as much as he could carry. So Dhantari discontinued his journey and returned home. The snake was happy because he knew that Dhantari was the only one in this world who could bring the Rajah back to life. So on the appointed day, the Rajah entered the steel cage with a strong guard all round. When he felt quite safe a woman offered him some plums—one of which contained a worm as any over-ripe fruit would. That worm was none other than Taksaka himself, who managed to enter the cage in this manner. As soon as the Rajah bit the plum that worm came out and grew into a tremendous size and bit the Rajah immediately who soon became like ashes. Then Taksaka disappeared. The Rajah's son was born soon after this event, and when he grew up to be a man and learnt the details of his father's death he took a vow that he would take his father's revenge. So accordingly one day, as a result of his supplications to the gods, all the snakes were made to gather together in his presence in order to be recognised, arrested and executed for the death of his father. Everyone was present except Taksaka. The son sent up the prayers to heavens with double vigour, with the result that Taksaka hid himself under the throne of Indra, the God of the Heaven. But the power of the Rajah's prayers was such that Indra's throne was twice dragged down to the earth. Indra asked the Rajah's son what he had done, that his throne should twice be brought down by force of prayers. Neither of them knew that Taksaka was hidden there or that it was on account of him that the throne came down two times. However, the Rajah's son did not consider it proper to bring down a god's throne while praying for Taksaka, so he let the matter go; and that is how Taksaka is still free to bite people and his poison is with great difficulty counteracted.

Now Dhantari died in Benares after some years, surrounded by his disciples. His last advice to them was that, in order to be perfect disciples of him and also to have the same power to counter act the effect of the bite of Taksaka, they should not burn his body but should instead make it into pieces and eat it. Accordingly they did as they were told and were ready to eat; when Taksaka, who realiz-ing that if they ate the flesh of old Dhantari they would be so many Dhantaris as his arch-enemies, appeared in the form of a Brahmin, and with great passion advised them to desist from such a course; for who had heard that chelas (disciples) ate the flesh of their own dead guru? This made a strong impression on them and they threw the body in the flowing water of the river. But down the river there were certain people who did eat Dhantari's flesh by rescuing it from the water, either by mistake or knowingly; and those people were called Motisagars, while chelas of Dhantari were called Dhantaris. Dhantaris are considered superior to Motisagars, both in status as well as in curing snake-bites. There are about two hundred Dhantaris in Nagpur District, and a larger number of the Motisagar brotherhood. It is not known how many of them are in the whole of the Central Provinces.

Whenever and wherever and whatever he may be doing, no sooner does a mantri of the Dhantari class (and I believe also of the Motisagar group) hear that some one has been bitten by a snake, than he runs to save the victim, no matter if he has to go for miles.

If a man is bitten within four or five months before the coming Nag Panchmi Festival, Dhantari stops the poison from rising up by 'band bandhna,' and waits and cures it permanently on the next Nag Panchmi Festival; but if one is bitten three or four months after this festival, then he does not let the victim wait for so many months, but cures him immediately. In the case of the former it does not mean that the victim waits in agony for so many months; practically speaking, he is cured but not permanently cured until he does 'band kholna' which means taking off the ligatures of mantras.

The mantras as the leading Dhantari told me are, strictly speaking, two only. When ligatures of mantras are used for stopping the poison, the mantras are said in the names of Mahadeo and Parbati ("Our Adam and Eve" as the man said) and they are taken off in the same way and in the same names. Passes of hands are made in one direction and in peculiar twisting manner for stopping the poison from rising up, and at the time of curing permanently the passes are made in the opposite way. It may be mentioned here that mantristic ligatures put by one Dhantari can be taken off (*i. e.*, permanently cured) by another Dhantari, but not by a Motisagar; though ligatures put by a Motisagar can be opened by a Dhantari. A Dhantari therefore is superior to a Motisagar. Now besides reciting the mantras in the names of Mahadeo and Parbati there are nine Khands—a long mantra with nine stanzas—which are also recited after a Bari has been sung. When poison has taken effect only in the body below the neck, only five stanzas are recited quite rapidly: but if the victim has reached a stage where he is no longer able to support himself, *i.e.*, if instead of falling on his face while standing, he has the tendency to fall on his back, then two more stanzas are sung in his ears. The *Dat phorna* is not done until after the fifth stanza is sung. When the mouth of the victim is closed and his jaws are stiff, the mantrist, with the help of other people, opens the jaws and forcibly puts his two fingers in his throat and takes out blocks of almost solidified and thick saliva or foam. This is called to break the block, or *Dat phorna.* The *Dat phorna* can be done only when the Khands are being sung. The victim has to stand on the leaves of a nim tree when the *Dat* is taken out, and he has to have a fresh change of leaves for every *Dat*, and at every *Dat* the victim is made to face a different direction. The eighth Khand is recited when there is no poison left in the body, and it is then that the mantristic ligature in the names of Mahadeo and Parbati are tied, which means that there will be no more rising of poison. After this, the victim is taken to the temple of the Monkey-god where cocoanuts are broken and camphor is pasted, and a bow made to the god. It is after this process that the ninth Khand or stanza is recited and the ligatures are opened. No fee is charged.

The Dhantaris claim that so long as the victim is standing and is not lying prostrate, they can cure him, no matter how poisonous the snake. But in the case of cobra bite, they can effect a cure only if the victim is brought to them immediately, within perhaps five minutes of the bite, which is not always possible. Further, Dhantaris say that the victim should not have been given any kind of medicine after the bite, as they are unable to do anything then. If medicine has been given only a few minutes before the victim is brought to them they make the victim vomit. A few instances were given of cases in which the victims died because of taking medicine first and coming to them afterwards !

They further declare that if a man is bitten even some ten miles from the nearest Dhantari, he can be brought down without the poison taking its effect, only if a hair knot is tied on the victim's head (which probably would be easier in the case of Hindus who have long top knots) and also if a stone slab is kept pressed against the knot until such time as he reaches a Dhantari. From the financial point of view, the smaller the stone the better, as the victim on getting cured is expected to distribute 'Jaggery' equal to the weight of the stone, among the people of the locality !

Dhantaris have their own difficulties also. They are expected to find out whether a person is really bitten or just pretending. For this purpose they keep in stock 'one anna worth of ammonia powder' which they can get from the bazar easily. They put a pinch of it near the victim's nose ; and this decides whether he or she is senseless or not.

The leading Dhantari told the author all the mantras, but requested him that they should not be put in writing, as they would then lose all effect. The Dhantari himself wanted to put them in writing but was advised by his father never to do so. The same Dhantari is willing, indeed anxious, to initiate the author into the Brotherhood. A person of any religion can be initiated into the mystery, which involves certain ceremonies such as taking bath in a stream, a little of sun worship, and a bow to the Monkey-god—which was an obstacle in the author's way in accepting the offer. And the most important thing for the Dhantari is the present, which he is enjoined never to ask for, though never to refuse if offered ! He further said that the initiated—generally poor—ordinarily offered him a pair of Dhotis but that as the author was 'a Burra Sahib', he would be able to give a much better present !

The sight of a snake-charmer is quite common in India. Does he not only exhibit his cobras and their dances, but serves another useful purpose also. In the house where there is a snake which cannot be either removed to a safe distance or killed, a snake charmer is called upon to play his weird and quaint music on the 'bean'—his musical instrument. The music is so enchanting to the snake that being charmed, he comes out of his hole and squats right in front of the charmer. After a little while when the music is at the highest pitch, it is stopped suddenly and abruptly. The snake is still there with raised hood but apparently without his senses. The charmer bags it and is off with his fee of a rupee or so. These people are generally immune against snake-bites. It is said that they eat certain herbs which counteract the poison. They either catch their own snakes or purchase them from the professional snake-catchers who are wonderfully immune against all kinds of snake-bites. They handle them as one handles doves. It may be mentioned in this connection that in the Siwalik Hills and the Himalayas young boys handle big, black scorpions, like toys. with the help of herbs which they keep chewing all the time they have the scorpions in their hands or about their body.

It is said that very old snakes, living undisturbed in the thick of jungles have a manka—a brilliant precious stone—in their head. At night time, when all is quiet, they come out and throw the stone out on a clear piece of ground. As it glows in the dark, the snake dances about in its light and seems to admire it. After he is satisfied, he sucks the stone back through the mouth and sticks it in its proper place in the head where it remains encrusted like a jewel. A Hindu, about eighty years old, who told the author of it, said that there are two ways in which the stone can be secured. One is to spread a thick layer of ashes on the place where a snake of this kind is accustomed to dance in the light of its gem. As he blows out the stone from his mouth, it sinks in the soft ashes and is lost to view of the snake. The second method is to sit on a nearby tree ready with a metal basin of the shape of a washing bowl, hung in an inverted manner face downward—by means of strings. As soon as the snake throws out the stone, this basin is immediately lowered and placed on it. When the only thing of which the snake is proud is lost, he gets wild through rage. He becomes almost blind with anger. He lashes himself on, or round about, the ashes area, or on the metal basin till he is dead through exhaustion. It is said that such a snake when his stone is lost never survives the shock. He is generally dead before the day breaks.

In India, the snake is one of those subjects on which anybody can talk, even children can say something interesting. Thousands die every year of snake bite, and there are millions in India who have sometime or other just escaped from being bitten. A chat about snakes is as absorbing and as interesting, and thrill—giving, as a tale about spirits, ghosts and thieves etc. If a group once starts talking on one of these subjects, story after story comes out from all quarters. The story ranges round deaths and escapes of people, bigness and poisonousness or otherwise of snakes. In such a group some one or other is sure to mention some particular snake living in a particular corner of a jungle, or in ruins of ancient buildings or in an old well—no longer used—of the time of the Moghul emperors, or old deserted temples, guarding treasures, generally gold mohurs, kept in big copper cooking pots (Degs). Such ones are always black snakes, considered to be very old having a few long hairs on the mane with blood shot eyes and emitting, when moving, a creaking sound as that created by an ordinary country shoe. It is a fact that treasures have been found within the jurisdiction of a black snake. It is quite probable that such snakes find quite a cosy resting place in the mouths of such degs. Such snakes are considered almost human, at least by a class of people, generally known as Nag Baroteys. One does not come across them very often, nor do they attract any great attention, except sometimes—as happened twice only in the case of the author—when one sees a magician-looking-sort of man drawing water from a well by means of a white thin rope and a brass pan, and then in a very dignified manner throwing a pice into the well as the payment to the snake for the water. Travelling through out-of-the-way places a Nag Barota wanders all over India, with a bag slung from his shoulder, rope and a lota, a stick, a blanket, a few leaves of paper and a *Been*—a musical instrument made out by hollowing a ripe pumpkin or gourd—a thing always possessed by a snake charmer. It is a mystery how they maintain a regular supply of money when they do not beg, and pay for every thing, even to nature and have no ostensible means of livelihood. It is generally believed that it is the snakes who are their treasurers and who pay them for not only reading to snakes their janam patri (horoscope) but also like the Mirasis read from manuscripts they have in their possession, an account of the doings and achievements of their (snakes) ancestors. These people are a sort of priests for the snake. Mirasis are the professional musicians—considered to be a low caste in India, generally found in the Punjab, who on certain occasions recite orally for payment of a small fee, with no written records for reference, the geneology of each man of the particular village of which the said Mirasi is a resident.

While at the subject of snakes, the author also, like other snakists would like to mention a couple of incidents in connection with the above subject which he thinks might be of some interest to the readers.

Some years ago, when the river Indus was in great floods, and was playing havoc round about Dera Ghazi Khan the snakes which had lived and flourished there in countless numbers away from the ravages of the Indus and were swarming in the cosy jungles, found themselves in a Noah's flood. For miles around nothing could be seen except water, and a few trees protuding out of it. The small boats which went about for rescue work found some of these small trees entirely covered with snakes of all sorts, hues, and descriptions, big and small—from the old sire to the wee bits. Leaves could hardly be seen, in fact, it was a strange and quiet creeping pandemonium. They were clustering round the trunk and the branches in folds upon folds —all moving, some passing from under each other, others upon the tails, some lying like warp and woof. Such trees looked quite alive and quivering like the trees in the desert under the tremendous heat of the equatorial sun. But it were not the trees only where they found shelter. They would try to climb into the boats by dozens and the men had to be constantly on the look-out to sweep them off into the water.

It was in the fields adjoining one of the tiny villages of the Siwalik Hills that one morning, after it had rained for a few hours and water was standing much more than ankle deep, all the black cobras crept upon the big stones that were lying scattered about in the field and there they basked under the gentle heat of the clouded sun. There were scores of them. It was a never to-be-forgotten sight. Most astonishing was the lightning quickness with which they in their anger would snap at, without missing the rebounding brick-bats and small pieces of stone which were being showered at them. There were two or three cobras on each stone and it was rarely that they were hit by brickbats and stones. In white rage, and in fury, their hoods up, they looked round very challengingly as if to ask who could be so foolish as to annoy them by throwing stones at them! Their quickness was beyond praise. After a few hours they all disappeared and the men resumed their work in the same field without giving much thought to them!

RAKSHABANDHAN

ANOTHER name of this festival is *Rakhi Bandhana.* It falls on the 15th of the month of Shravan; *i.e.*, on the day of the full-moon of this month. On this day the people, especially the traders living on the seashore, offer cocoanuts to the sea-god, in order to praise him, as well as to seek protection for their merchandise on ships. This is called Narali-Purnima. There are two other ceremonies which also take place the same day. One is the ceremony of changing the Jenao—sacred thread, which is compulsory for all Brahmins; and the day is called *Shravni.* There are one or two other festivals also on which the sacred cord may be changed, such as Pola, the festival of cattle, which falls a fortnight later.

It is said that on Rakshabandhan day the brave take a pledge to protect the weak and the poor.

On this day, rings of thread, twisted a given number of times, are also prepared and offered to the triumvirate, Shiva, Vishnu and Brahma. But in North-West India this day is observed by the people in a different way. They tie on each other's wrists ringlets of coloured silk thread twisted with a little of tinsel thread, and knotted every half inch or so, with pieces of extra thread and tinsel, to look like tiny tassels; so that the whole thing appears like a miniature garland of flowers. Now this is done to wish each other prosperity and well-being during the coming year. The word 'raksha' means good or well-being and bandhana—to tie. The wife of Indra, the king of the heavens, prayed to Vishnu for such an amulet for her husband, who was afraid of Bali, the king of the nether-land (hell) and obtained it, thereby securing protection against Bali. Similarly, the people do it to get protection from evil. They are greatly afraid of this demon-king, who is the king of the darkness. In India, the houses of Hindus are lit immediately it gets dark. No moment is lost in this respect. No sooner is it dark than the lamps are lighted in the house; otherwise King Bali would take possession and cast an evil influence on it. Even the houses which are just built and are not dry enough to move into, are lit every evening in order to keep off Bali's evil influence. The author has often noticed mothers rebuking their grown-up daughters, or mothers-in-law their daughters-in-law, if even a little delay has taken place in the lighting of the lamps. And for the very same reason some good soul goes and lights even the deserted shrines, and the tiny wayside temples which are veritable doll-houses.

The Guru or the teacher ties this wristlet round the boy's wrist with a mantra, which says in effect, that he may be saved from the evil influence of Bali. Now, men tie it on each other's hand, the wife ties on her husband's wrist, the mother on her son's, sisters on their brothers'. Women do not wear it, probably due to the reason that the wife of Indra got this amulet for her husband, and not for herself, When a guru ties this amulet round his chela's wrist, the chela has to pay a fee of a few annas. This custom of tying wristlets is very popular among Marwaris. While others use just one such ringlet, the Marwaris do not mind more than one. So on this day, and on the next day, which can also be kept as Rakshabandhan Day, the Brahmins throng round the men who sit ready with a lot of change. For every wristlet they pay so much money. While their wrists are quite thick with scores of such wristlets, the Brahmins return home after running about the whole day with pockets full of money. This custom is very popular among Marwaris.

Rakshabandhan is also called *Rukhi Poli.* Rakhi means golden paper. Amulets made of golden paper and imitation pearls are tied round children's arms. This is not done in the case of grown-ups; for them only the tasselled wristlets are used. On this day it is a familiar sight to see boys going about in clean and bright clothes with wristlets tied round their wrists and munching away at eatables specially prepared for the occasion.

NARALI PURNIMA

THIS Festival of "Cocoanut Throwing in the Sea" falls on the 15th day of Sravan, *i.e.*, on full-moon day. The ceremony is performed especially by the West Coast people, largely in Bombay and Goa, and also, perhaps on the East Coast; the idea being to keep the sea calm and smooth. In the rainy season the sea is generally rough and high, the south-west winds blow and bring storms. Hence the commercial classes are naturally anxious for the safety of their ships and also for the cargo. But some say that from this date the south-west monsoon is on the decline; hence there is an anticipated joy of safety to ships and trade in general. But it is not only the traders who are interested in it, but also the sea-faring people who undertake the hazards of difficult voyages. Traders think that by offering cocoanuts, flowers, betel and betelnuts, they will please the sea-goddess or god who will keep them safe from all financial loss which they might incur through rough seas and storms. The sailors do it to ensure their personal safety.

Crowds of people—men, women and children—attired in their holiday dress, go to the seashore early in the morning (though in some places it is done in the afternoon) either to watch the fun or perform the ceremony. The traders are ready on the shore with thousands of bags of cocoanuts, flowers, garlands and other things. The sailors and boatwallas go about in their little tubs in holiday dress; in fact, this is the only festival which sailors can call as their own.

They throw the offerings into the sea with shouts of praises to the god or the goddess, or to the festival itself. They throw money also, according to their means, from one pice to sovereigns. As they throw these things they utter a few words of prayer but without the help of Brahmins. The cocoanuts which do not float away far into the sea are gathered together by the poorer people who lie in wait for them. When the primary function of cocoanut-throwing is duly gone through, nobody cares who secures the offerings, because those are then the 'left-over' of the gods. One can see lots of urchins and grown-ups loitering about in the water for this purpose like the boot-leggers. They organize themselves into parties and while some secure their booty in battle royal, others are on the shore to receive it and hand it over in turn to the depot a few yards behind. Of course the loot is divided when all is over. After a short time one sees nothing but garlands idly floating on the surface. But by no means the best food is given to the gods, at least on this occasion. A special effort is made to buy the cheapest lot in the bazaar, which means either they are very small or very bad; generally the latter.

The sailors' songs and ditties on this occasion are worth hearing. They ply the oars as they go singing in groups. The songs have a peculiar rhythm which gives additional incentive to ply more energetically, all at the same time, with a minimum of exertion. The tunes are wild and weird, classic and romantic, and unparalleled in beauty. These are special songs, sung either in praise of the sea or of the goddess.

As for the origin of this festival, nothing is given in the scriptures but it is likely that whoever started it, must have done so in connection with the goddess of water, and if he happened to be a trader or a sailor or an owner of ships, and a victim of losses at sea, he probably tried to draw the attention of the goddess by throwing a "bait" in the sea, and so to appease or please her; and thus he secured the satisfaction of the belief that the goddess would have mercy on his ships and cargo.

POLA

THIS is the festival of Cattle, observed in different parts of India on different dates. The owners of cattle are anxious to give them a happy time at least once a year; especially the bullocks whose bodies are decorated with marks and designs of different colours, their horns with tassels and golden papers, and their necks with necklaces of beads, or copper or brass bells. Those who can afford to do so make beautiful and bright-coloured coats also for them. The bullocks are washed and rubbed in the morning; but then they are retied to their posts, instead of getting ready for the day's labour. Surely the bullocks seem to wink and feel surprised! Then after enjoying this annual sabbath till four o'clock in the afternoon, the bullocks are taken to an appointed place where all the other bullocks gather together in a sort of *mela* (fair). They are all made to stand in a line. On the command being given and incited by music, they are made to run—wildly—and all together, which results in a furious stampede, followed by their owners. It is like pandemonium let loose. The spectacle of men shouting at the top of their voices and running along hidden by the clouds of dust raised by the noisy patter of hundreds of hoofs, and the clanging of scores of copper and brass bells, is thrilling. No one dare come in front of this surging mass of cattle, unless he wants to commit suicide! They all run together a furlong or so, and then the men along with their respective bullocks begin taking different directions. These bullock-drivers are generally farmers, cart-drivers and in many cases working as servants in the hire of others. These people drive their oxen to their respective masters, patrons and friends, and ask alms and presents on behalf of their dumb companions. The author's washerman would always come to his door, dragged by his diminutive ox, and beg for some bakhshish.

In the house, women-folk worship the cows and mark them with red powder on their foreheads to show that they—cows—are not widows but still enjoying the bliss of married life! Cows are considered sacred in the house of a Hindu. They are looked after as if they were members of the family. And the cows of India do respond to the kindly feeling of their Hindu masters; they are so docile, that a cow will come and stand near the children who will rub her forehead and will not be afraid. In India the wandering cattle are allowed great liberty. They go about in the streets unmolested, and are as free to go about in the bazaars as men. The passing Hindu on the street considers it good to touch a passing cow with his hand and he does it 'instinctively'. So long as these good cattle do not block the roads against cars and other vehicles, non-Hindus also respect them!

The cow is, moreover, called Gau Mata—mother cow, for she gives milk, curd, butter and ghee. She supports the earth on her horns. She is the main prop of the farmers. To kill a cow is an unforgiveable sin, and woe to the man or woman who kills one even inadvertently; he will have to undergo a long and painful penance for it. A Hindu will never sell his cow to a butcher. A butcher is generally a Mohammedan. Still, there are Hindu butchers also, and at the time of the writing of this article a case is being tried in a court of the Central Provinces whether a Hindu butcher is an 'untouchable or not. So a Hindu in place of giving his cow to a butcher will keep her for her life-time, whether she gives any milk or not. No consideration is paid to the economic loss thus involved. Those Hindus who are no longer able to keep a dry and old cow send her to a Home for cows—called Gau Shala which is maintained by Hindu charities. Every town and city in India possesses such Homes. To give *dan*—alms in charity—to such a home helps a great deal in attaining *moksha* or salvation. The cows have come to be regarded as sacred apparently through usefulness.

In South India, on this day, cooked rice is given to the cows and are worshipped by men and women. In some of the criminal tribes of South India, a girl lays down as a condition of marriage that whosoever will forcibly remove from the horns of a rogue bull the precious thing wound round his horns, will secure her hand. For this purpose, at the usual meeting place of the festival, the prospective bridegrooms gather together to fulfil the condition. They generally succeed, as the girls know they will. This is a great occasion for the people and they remember it for months.

JANAM ASHTAMI

(Krishnashtami or Gokul Ashtami)

THERE is a tradition among the Hindus that whenever the wicked annoy and persecute the righteous for their righteousness, God undertakes an incarnation, not only to fight for them, but also to save the world from destruction imminent on account of their evil deeds. Krishna, the eighth avatar or incarnation, came to the world for this purpose, and also in response to the prayers of Vasudeo who wanted to see him.

Devaki, a cousin of Kauns or Kamsa, King of Muttra, was married to Vasudeo of the Chandra Bansi family, or Lunar race. On the marriage day, the king drove the couple in his own chariot, and took them in a procession through the streets. As the royal procession was passing, a voice from heaven addressed Kauns and said that the eighth child of Devaki would kill him. Now Kauns was a most unpopular and cruel king; and the people having got tired of his tyranny, prayed to be saved from his unjust rule. So when Kauns heard these words he became angry. and determined to kill Devaki immediately, but when Vasudeo promised to hand over all his children to him, he desisted. The first six children were delivered into his hand to be murdered, but the seventh, and the eighth who was Kirshna,* escaped.

At the time of Kirshna's birth, Vasudeo seized him in his arms, and under the hooded protection of Sesha Nag, the snake, he passed out of the palace gate without being observed by the guard, who was fast asleep. This happened at dead of night, when the rain was pouring heavily and the river Jumna was full and flowing furiously. As he entered the river to cross (some say it became knee-deep) the hanging feet of Krishna touched the water, whereupon it parted into two, and thus they walked across on the dry bed with the walls of water on both sides.

Now across the river in the village of Gokul, a female child was also born at the same time as Krishna, to Jasoda, the wife of Nanda, a cowherd. Before the woman returned to her senses, the children were exchanged and the girl brought to the palace, where she cried. The guards hearing it, hastened to inform the king, who came immediately

* Krishna can be recognized in current pictures by his blue complexion. He wears a coronet on his head, has four hands, and holds in each hand respectively a conch shell, a staff, a sharp white discus whirling round one of his fingers, and a flute. He stands on a lotus-flower, and the soles of his feet are marked with the same flower.

to kill her but before he could do so, the child slipped from his hands and went up like lightning, laughing and saying "O Fool! the boy, thine enemy, is born elsewhere; take care!"; and disappeared. Thereupon the king, full of wrath, ordered that every strong and newly-born male child in the kingdom should be put to death, and sent his men in all directions for this purpose.

When he came to know of a child in Gokul who was wonderfully strong and active, he sent his man for him in disguise. That man went to the door of Nanda's house in the guise of a Brahmin to beg. As usual, the beggar Brahmin uttered the words of blessing saying 'May God make you a Raja,' and so on, and thereupon the wooden cradle on which Krishna was lying went flying towards him and hit him. This man whose name was Mamam Bhatji, informed Kauns of what had happened.

On hearing of this, the king became very sad and said that Krishna, as a mere child, was already playing havoc, and when he would grow up to be a man he would be uncontrollable. However, years passed by, and one day, in full Durbar, Krishna came in, looking a mere child to the eyes of all except Kauns himself to whom he looked like a huge giant. He went to him, sprang upon his chest and killed him with his sword in front of the full assembly. He then took the reins of government in his own hands, and from there proceeded to Dwarka which he built for the people of Mathura.

In order to worship Krishna whose other names are Kanoba, Girdhari, Kunjbehari, Bensriwala, Kanhiyya, people buy his idol ready-made from the bazaar or make it at home. Armed with his 'weapons' he is placed in the middle of a small wooden table which is kept on a place nicely plastered-over with cowdung. Besides his flute he holds a laddu (sweet-meat ball) also in one of his hands. Being a child, he is naturally pleased to have this 'sweet'. The table is surrounded by flower-pots, and the idol is sprinkled over with red powder and scent. A tiny oil lamp is also placed by the image. Men and women worship together with the help of the necessary materials of worship, and are guided by a Brahmin priest, who is paid four to eight annas as his fee, and invited to the feast next morning, to which friends and relatives are also invited. This worship is conducted at twelve o'clock at night. Previous to it for three or four hours the account of Krishna's birth is recited to the congregration collected for the purpose, and is timed to finish just at midnight, when the book is closed rather abruptly in order that the audience might proceed to worship. It may be mentioned that the following things are distributed among the congregation, as 'parshad':— parched maize or dhan, pounded rice, cucumber, curd, mango pickle, juice of sugarcane and chillies. The reason for this is that Krishna in his boyhood, when out grazing the cattle, used to collect the other cowherd-boys and make them put their food in the midst to be shared by all, thus enabling everybody to enjoy different things. This way of collecting food together is called Gopal Kala. This account of Krishna's life is repeated year after year.

The same night and the next morning also, the idol is placed in a beautiful cradle which is swung while the girls sing a lullaby to put the child Krishna to sleep. Right above the cradle, within the reach of child Krishna, hangs what is called a Pholora—a framework of four wooden sticks tied to each other in crosswise fashion. On the joint of these sticks hang by threads all the delicious things which the worshipper can procure or prepare for pleasing him, so that Krishna may have just to stretch out his hand in order to eat whatever his taste demands. Iron Pholoras can be had ready-made from bazaars.

On the evening of Janam Ashtami day the idols of Krishna are taken in procession, with singing and music, to a stream or a tank where they are immersed in water. In a small town, the idols owned by rich men, generally made of silver, are taken to the tank on picturesque chariots decorated with plantain-leaves and flower-pots, and drawn by a team of painted bullocks. A procession of a large number of such picturesque chariots carrying shining silver images preceeded by Indian bands and halting by the side of a big tank surrounded by huge banyan trees, produces an impression which is not soon forgotten. It looks like a 'dream of the East'. Before immersion the idols are taken to a boat specially made for the purpose which takes them round for a 'joy-ride' before consigning them to oblivion for at least a year. This boat is generally made of big rafters tied together. On it a hut of banana leaves and other green foliage is built and brilliantly lighted. This looks very beautiful in the darkness. The silver idols are then restored to their different chariots which are stationed in front of the tank temple; and there people pass from chariot to chariot, bowing.

In the Central Provinces, the Mahars sow wheat in baskets some eight days before the birthday, and as they take the clay images to be thrown in the stream, they take along these baskets. When the mud is washed off the roots of the pale-coloured sprouts, they bring them back, some to be kept in the place of the image, and the rest to be exchanged with friends as symbols of greetings.

The festival of Krishna is the only one of two or three festivals which come in the dark half of a month, the others being Shivratri and Devali. Krishna himself was dark-blue in complexion. And darkness came on this world by his death; for Kali Yuga began with his death.

Rukmini was his wife and Radha his Love. More praises are sung of Radha than his wife. In the North it is Radha who is mentioned with his name. In the Central Provinces, especially among the Mahars, young boys form themselves into a party, and go dancing with music, through the streets. Both old and young, men and women, enjoy it tremendously and are greatly excited. They enjoy particularly the rhythmic dance, in which the dancers use short multi-coloured sticks, striking them together while dancing in a ring and in different formations; the striking of sticks keeps time with the stamping of feet which are covered with anklets of tiny brass bells. At frequent intervals a man somewhere on the outskirts of the crowd fires a rocket, which immediately brings the dancing party to its knees. Then the leader of the group shouts 'Krishna Maharaj ki jai' and the party is up on its feet again and goes on dancing as before. This party exhibits its art from house to house of those friends, acquintances and others who are likely to give some bakhshish.

Krishna, as the most popular incarnation of Vishnu, is worshipped all over India though under different names. He was born in the Rohini asterism and killed his maternal uncle. So if a boy is born in the same asterism, his maternal uncle (if he has any) does not feel very happy at his birth. In former days such children were put to death; but in these days a maternal uncle is just superstitiously careful and is teased by his friends.

In some parts of Central India, especially in the C. P. and Berar, the ceremoney of the birth of Krishna is observed in another way also. On this day a pitcher full of curd is hung on a tree some eight feet above the ground, under which both the old and the young dance vigorously for two hours before the birth of Krishna, which takes place exactly at midnight. At this time the dancers break the pitcher as they dance beneath it, and the curd that falls on them is caught in their hands and eaten as *prasad.* The whole thing is taken more as a joke than as a serious religious ceremony. It may be noted that curd, butter and milk were the things which were greatly relished by Krishna in his boyhood in Gokul where he was brought up among herdsmen.

Mention may be made here of the boyish pranks of Krishna. They are recounted among the old and the young, with enjoyment. He has endeared himself to millions of simple folk in this manner. He is remembered as the leader of the boys who followed him with unswerving zeal and faithfulness. He was particularly fond of curd and buttor and in the effort to secure these would go to any lengths. He would set out on such petty expeditions well armed with the necessary weapons of stealing, which were a thick stick, sand, ground chillies and thorns. These weapons he used only for defending himself in awkward situation. The sand he would throw into the eyes of any who came upon him in the act of stealing. If he wanted just a second to clear off he would throw sand, but for a long period he would throw chillies which were more effective. The thorns he would spread on the way if anyone chased him in order to gain a start every time the chaser bent down to pick out one from the sole of his or her feet. He used to go on such expeditions either along with a group of clever boys or alone.

GANESH CHATURTI

GANESH Chaturti falls on the fourth of the bright half of the month of Bhadarpad or Bhadon. It is related to the worship of Ganesh.

The following story gives one origin of the festival. Once all the gods decided to go and see the God Shiva, whose usual abode is Kailas Parbat in the Himalayas. As usual Bramha rode on a swan, Shiva on a bull, Vishnu on an eagle and, Ganpati had his rat to ride upon.

Just at the time of climbing the Kailas an accident happened which brought trouble on poor Moon (Chandra). In their excitement of climbing up Ganpati slipped off his rat and fell down. The other gods did not notice it except one god, Moon, who indiscreetly smiled; probably he could not help it as the spectacle must have been a funny one—Ganpati with a big belly, unmanageable body, short stature, face of an elephant with a trunk—rolling down the slope in a distressful manner. And Ganesh cursed him in his rage and said: "Those who look at thy face shall be accused of a crime because of thy foul face; those who look at thee shall be looked down upon as corrupt fellows." When Chandra heard this he was greatly grieved, and so were the other gods. And Chandra attended by all the others went up to Ganpati and begged for mercy. After a long time Ganpati took pity upon him and took back his curse, but with one reservation. "I pardon you this time," he said, "but the effect of this curse will prevail one day in the year." And that day is Ganesh Chaturti. On this particular day no one should look at the moon, and if one happens to see it by mistake, the best way to ward off the effect of the curse is to commit a minor offence purposely, and so save oneself from being accused of a more serious one, committed perhaps unawares. Now the mischief which is commonly and deliberately committed is the throwing of stones and brick-bats on to the roofs of houses. The sufferers abuse the offenders and the offenders are pleased in turn as they are not accused of anything more serious. Breakable things are generally moved inside the house at this time and so people do not take this matter of stone-throwing seriously; they expect it; in fact, they do it themselves. The weathar is generally fine, the moonlight is clear, and the fun is great. One hears a great hue and cry, and the inmates come up on to the roofs of their houses, and enquire of each other as to who could be so foolish as to do such a thing. Then they rush to the door steps—in the streets, abusing at the top of their voices—using *gali* (billingsgate)—pure and unadulterated, sometimes funny curious, sometimes very dirty and studied. They shout in anger, and then stop suddenly as they hear a great crash on a roof in the neighbourhood; they begin again. Presently perhaps one of the fellows in the lane is hit, more anger—more shouts—then there is a lull for a few minutes, then a tremendous crash again. So on it begins again. Finally they have all gone in one by one, and they all guess the direction from which the stones are coming on to their roofs. 'They know, a certain man has two grown-up sons. They are mischievous too' 'The other has four sons and they are great rogues,' and so on. Most complacently, he, who thinks has been wronged, takes two or three clogs off the mud walls or picks up a few stones from the corner of his courtyard, and with all his might throws them in different directions and is satisfied; then he goes into his house and bolts it; and so does everyone. A very pandemonium is let loose; but slowly it dies down, and by midnight they are in bed, then quiet reigns supreme.

Now one might think that grown-ups, "educated men and cultured" would be free from such things. But no; the author, has heard them, in the street, criticizing such customs in a most indignant manner, but as soon as they have gone in, they also have enjoyed a few moments of boyishness by throwing stones in all directions in order to be let off the curse so easily. This day is humourously called Dagri Chauth also—the fourth of the stones—the day on which people throw stones at each other's houses.

This day people go to bazaar and buy an idol of Ganpati (those who cannot afford to buy, make one out of clay at home) and worship him at home.

It is said in the "traditions" that the period of keeping and worshipping the god at home should be a month and a half; but in practice some people keep it for five days, some for seven days, some for ten, and some for twenty-one days; others go to the extreme of keeping it throughout the year till they bring in a new idol of Ganpati, when they dispose off the old one by throwing it into a river, or tank. Together with the idol of Ganpati an idol of a rat is also shown, sitting on its hind legs and eating a laddu (sweet balls) with his forelegs. It has been mentioned above that the rat is Ganesh's vehicle. It is a grand day for rats. Nobody molests them and they take advantage of this day! They are bolder than usual, and perhaps they wonder why men's nature should change so suddenly!

Laddus (sweet preparation made like golf balls) are kept in different corners of the house—under the boxes, behind the pitchers and other earthenware—to allow rats to have their annual feast undisturbed. The author has seen people keeping platefuls of such sweets in the middle of the floor where, after a short time, one sees only broken residue and droppings.

This is not a day on which, like many other festivals, one has to observe a fast and eat nothing but fruits and milk! One may eat anything one likes including fruits and milk! In some places, people do keep a fast on this day; in fact, they do so on the fourth of every month.

People generally eat *modak* this day—a preparation greatly liked by Ganpati. Twenty-one of them are kept apart in a plate and offered first to Ganpati and then shared by the people. Ganpati is supposed to eat them and whatever is left over (which are still 21) is eaten by the people. Ganpati will be angry if not offered first.

The whole of this day is devoted to merry-making: go where you will, you find singing and music. The faces of the passers-by in the bazaars show happiness and joy; children jump about in bright coloured clothes, and their mouths are full of sweets. In the bazaar one finds *kirtans* or Bhajans (reading and singing of epics) going on at different places, the reader or singer sitting with his book on a coloured cushion placed on a raised place, with marks on his forehead and garlands on his neck, flowers lying scartered about the book, incense sticks burning on both sides of the table—the rich and the poor squating round on a big durrie—distinguished guests probably sitting near the reciter, resting on big clean white cushions. Brass plates full of *pan supari* (betel, nut) and cardamoms going round, and special pan-packets covered with silver leaves being passed to the distinguished guests. In another corner of the street one may find a pretty dancing-girl singing in front of a wealthy man's house amid a similar setting. One corner of the carpet is reserved for the dancing-girl where she sits down after every song, she is offered a pan-packet, chews it a while and spits it out in a special brass receptacle called *thook--dan*—of the shape of a vase with upper end flattened out. She gets up, sings and dances, followed by a *tabalchi* (drummer), by a *saringiwala* who plays at violin specially adapted for Indian music. As she dances they follow her from one end of the carpet to the other. They dare not get in front—they are quick to recede behind her when she turns about towards them. She is dressed in a pretty and costly saree, nice stockings, and shoes covered with gold work, wears gold ornaments on her wrists and neck, her hair is beautifully done up, and there is antimony round her eyes to make them more deer-like. The violinist is not so elaborately dressed up, but his beard often tends to excel the length of the violin itself. One may see his eyes half closed, his face contracting or expanding according to the rhythm of the music, neck hanging down. But he is the man who is called *ustad* or teacher, for he teaches her to sing scientifically. The *tabalchi* is a good looking- fellow. He has narrow trousers sticking to his legs tightly up to the knees and then they open up in many gatherings to give prominence to the thighs. This is gathered and secured through at the waist by a tape of silk threads which can stretch up to 12 inches in width. The two ends of this tape hang loose down to his knees. It is always of bright colours and ever keeps moving and peeping below the shirt. He wears a bright coloured or white vest and above it a long shirt of very thin muslin. Gold or silver chains with tiny bells take the place of buttons at the neck. One will find his moustaches curled up and cheeks carefully shaved—dark and long curly hair on his head and on it worn a small round cap worked all round with flowers of pure gold threads. It is tilted to the right or the left according to the whim of the man. The man is generally fair and handsome. He is usually a man of about thirty, and a popular favourite.

The method of worship is more or less the same as in all worship *i.e.*, Brahmins' fee, flowers, rice, cocoanuts, red powder, a lamp and a brass plate to wave in front of the idol, etc. During the festival days Ganpati is worshipped three times a day. Just as *bel* leaves are essential for Shiva worship, so are *shami* leaves for him. He is as fond of being besmeared with red powder as Hanuman the monkey-god who carried a mountain on his right hand. It may be noted that the worship of Ganesh entails a lot of expense. People go beyond their means to offer him the choicest of sweets which, of course, are eaten by the family and friends. They hold him in dread, for he is a jealous god and can't bear to see other gods being worshipped with more pomp and show. This day he has a special room, often a big public hall where he is seated on a small platform surrounded by flower-pots and coloured bulbs, his neck full of garlands offered by the worshippers. In front sit the musicians with their *sitar*, harmonium, drum and cymbals, who sing in his praise. They begin with "Do *namaskar* (obeisance) to the Ganpati Ganesh" The hall is very tastefully decorated. The author has seen few such big crowds as gather for his worship, for he is the giver of happiness. He is the most familiar of gods. You find him in every nook and corner. On this day he is seen sitting under a gorgious canopy with twenty-one blades of *durba* grass on his head. He has a most imposing personality.

It is very difficult to say who Ganesh was, because he is not mentioned in the great scriptures of the Hindus, but there are a few popular legends, though a bit confusing. The great God Shiva had gone out when his wife Parvati or Gauri began to take a bath in the countryard. As she rubbed her body she collected the dirt which had come off and made an idol of it, and infused life into it. She at once directed him to go and stand at the door and allow no one to come in while she took her bath. The sage Narad went and informed Shiva that his wife had given birth to a son (an illegitimate one). On hearing this, Shiva returned home and saw this lad standing at the door; and he would not permit even Shiva himself to enter; of course, poor Ganesh had not seen his father and so was not able to recognize him. In his rage the father cut off the head of his own son, and went inside the house to hear the true story. On hearing it, in order to please Parvati who was sorely grieved over the whole incident and who had also prayed for the restoration of his son's life, he promised to replace Ganpati's head with that of the first animal he came across. As an elephant was the first one he met, Ganesh was fitted with an elephant's head. Another version is that Parvati had created one son and one daughter—Ganesh and Usa—out of the dirt of her perspiration. At the time of the incident outside the door, the daughter was hiding in a *martaban* or a cask of salt. This day is another of those days on which people—generally women—do not use salt. They try to abstain from it as much as possible in deference to the life-saving quality of salt as was shown in this particular instance.

But to resume; the restoration of life and the fitting of an elephant's head was not enough. The beautiful face changed into an elephant head would not satisfy any mother; so, in order to satisfy her and show sympathy with her he enjoined that every human being, even the gods themselves should pay homage to him; and he further ordered that he should be given the first homage when anything is done by anybody. He made Ganesh even the controller of the breath of life. He has his elder brother also, Kartik, with six faces who, though worshipped, is not paid that respect which should be due to the elder brother of the most pampered god; even in his own household. Ganesh was given precedence over him. He was respected more than Kartik.

He is taken to be *Vigneswara*, the 'remover of difficulties and obstacles'. Those who are poor and are in sore need of financial help worship him, generally, either on the fourth of *shudh* (light half) or on the *budh* (dark half) of every Hindu month. They have to fast that day, which they break only after they have seen the moon. Cultivators are particularly anxious to worship him on this day as the festival takes place somewhere near the harvest when rains might affect them for better or for worse. But they are not the only people who do so; in fact, both the rich and the poor are eager to worship him as the fate of crops affects all. Naturally this festival is observed by every caste and sect—low and high. It is significant when cultivators, sitting in groups under a *peepul* tree, discussing the prospects of a harvest, interlace their talks with such expressions as these "if Ganesh Maharaj keeps it, etc., etc."

If one were to enter the premises of a big landlord or a nobleman, one would see on the gate posts two fine images of Ganpati—one on each post, that is to say, that one enters with all good omen. Inside the drawing room of a middle class house one would see in the niche on top of the door leading into the room a small image of Ganpati. In another house one would find two pictures of Ganpati painted on either side of the main door that opens in the street. On the top of documents one sees his name written first. New business is started with a worship to Ganesh. Ganpati's day is reserved for all things that are to be begun as first ventures. Start on a journey, open a shop, get engaged, get married, open a public library, open a new school, start erecting a building; for all this it is very auspicious this day. When you open an account book, write a letter, and even write an examination paper, write his name first on the top. On Divali, when performing Lakshmi Puja (the worship of the Goddess of Wealth) the name of Ganesh is tho first to be mentioned. When new accounts are opened "Sri Ganesh" is written in conspicuous letters on the top. A father sends his son to school for the first time on this day. Ganpati is regarded as the God of Learning also. This is a great day for school boys. The orthodox teacher in the primary school takes his class round to the houses of the pupils and the boys sing in praise of Ganesh and perform, a sort of folk-dance with multi-coloured wooden sticks held one in each hand. The boys—generally little fellows—move round in circle, striking the sticks in time to the tune, each boy striking together his own sticks, then the sticks of his fellow on the right, then the one in front, then crosswise, and so on. Then every other boy dances with a round-about turn when his fellows on the right and on the left have turned to their right and left respectively to strike the sticks and so on. Then they separate into small groups ; a boy stands in the middle, and the process is repeated in some other way; after a little while the singing is stopped, but the sticks go on and the rhythmical striking of the sticks retains in the mind the ordered continuity of the song or the tune. The boys perform the thing over at every house and the present—generally a minimum of one rupee—is given in each house which, of course, goes into the pocket of the teacher.

In many village schools one may find an idol of Ganesh in a niche behind the teacher's chair, in front of which every morning before the school begins the boys come and stand with folded hands and sing songs in praise of Ganesh. School and college students particularly regard him as their own god and use him in many ways, in studies or in politics. Ganesh Chaturthi, for instance, gives an added zest to the 'politically inclined' in Maharashtra.

Ganesh is a married god, his wife is Saraswati, the Vidya Devi, the Goddess of Learning with four hands. Her vehicle is a peacock.

The following are some of the names of Ganesh :—*Ganapati* (master of the Ganas, the attendants on Shiva), *Gajanan* (one who has the face of an elephant), *Vikra-tond* (one with a distorted face), *Vigna Hartha* (one who takes away pain), *Gaja karan* (one with the ears of an elephant), *Lambodar* (one with a big belly), *Vigna Nasha* (the destroyer of pain), *Ganadhpati*—(gana = necklace, adhpati = chief, that is, the chief pearl in the necklace made of gods; in other words, the loveliest and biggest gem among the gods), *Sudhi Devta* (the giver of success). *Vidyadhar* (one who holds learning), *Adyagan* (the first in the garland of gods), and *Vidyasagar* (the sea of knowledge).

His knowledge knows no bounds; for he is well versed in the 64 different arts ; in drawing, reading and writing, painting, in carpenter's, blacksmith's, tailor's, goldsmith's crafts, etc. He can also swim.

He knows the six Shastras, *i.e.*, the six sciences, including Physics, Chemistry, Biology, Astronomy,

Astrology, Mathematics, Philosophy. He knows all about electricity and wireless! One thing more and that is that he is a very fast writer. No matter how fast you dictate, he is always waiting with his pen ready to take down more and that in the long hand too. In order to compile the Vedas, Vyasa asked Ganpati to put them in black and white as he dictated. To his utter surprise Vyasa always found him waiting for more. Ganpati found him too slow.

One week before this festival, girls dressed in pretty saries go to temple with a small basketful of wheat sprouts. They go in groups, accompanied by music, and return in the same way after *puja* (worship). On the day of the festival, within the reach of the god is hung a *pholora*—three small sticks tied crosswise on four other sticks of the same size, each a few inches apart; from this net-work are hung choicest fruits and sweets—so that he may just stretch out his hands to help himself with anything he likes. Of course, the members of the household polish off the whole thing later on.

After the festival is over, the image of Ganpati is carried to a river or tank in procession and children shout Ganpati, Ganpati Morya; Pudhalya Varshi Lavakar Ya—*Marhatti*—meaning, Oh! Ganpati, come soon next year. Every family has the ambition to instal an amage of Ganpati in its house though every one cannot afford to do so, being quite an expensive affair. So people instal one in their particular Mohalla or locality where they congregate in the evenings and sing his praises and distribute *pans* to guests and friends. Even non-Hindus are invited to partake such marks of friendship. The image is kept far inside on a platform specially erected in the centre of the floor. Between the door of the room and the image are erected one after another at a distance of one foot each, rectangular openings like doors, made of white thick paper cut in beautiful filigree work and formed into delicate tracery. Lights near the image make these papers look from outside like marble work inside the Taj at Agra. If the lamp behind has a chimney of blue colour, the effect on the paper gates is simply marvellous! It is like seeing a fairy house in dreamland. If seen from the front and in proper perspective one wonders if the whole thing is real. The roof of this heavenly avenue is covered with blue tiny bulbs which look like stars in the firmament. The layer upon layer of heavens reminded the author of the Mohammedan belief that there are seven layers or Tabaqs of heavens. It is not necessary that his image should be installed in the manner given above. People do so in scores of different ways.

These images are carried to the tank in procession either with music or with choirs of singers who as they sing strike tiny cymbals. The rich carry the image to the tank with great pomp and show, and in true oriental style. Passing through the quaint eastern bazaars, headed by a band of Indian pipers and drummers, all dressed in turbans of blazing colours and long and flowing coats of thin white material, rather tightly wound Dhotis (loin cloth) and turned up, red heel-less shoes, there come the duly caparisoned horses, with thick necklaces and garlands of pure siver, unridden and accompanied at either side by quaintly dressed men carrying glistening tasselled spears; then follow similarly attired camels, who like serene philosophers thud along with measured steps. The men sitting on top keeping rhythmic movement with the necks of camels; then come elephants beautifully painted on the fourehead and, on the whole, nicely decorated, and these are accompanied by what look like narrow ladders. These ladders about 15 to 20 feet in length have receptacles attached to every rung that contains oil seeds or oil which are lighted. Each ladder is carried by two men lengthwise, parallel to the road, one on either side of the road, leaving the road between the two vacant. Immediately after these lighted ladders are carried in gaily decorated phaetons or palanquins the image or images of Ganpati and his wife wearing costly necklaces and other jewellery, brilliantly reflecting the brilliant lights around them. The inside of the phaeton or palanquin is generally fitted with flower pots and large looking glasses. There are besides quite a number of gas lamps also which are carried on the heads of coolies, throwing a flood of light on Ganpati and on the master of the whole show who sits beside the image in gorgeous dress. The other members of his family come in carriages following the image. These carriages are followed by standard bearers and others, in number between two and three scores of men dressed in quaint uniforms carrying spears and shields of olden days and followed by more ladder lights and gas lights. In a big city such processions begin coming out from five in the evening and go on passing one after another till 10 p.m., when they begin to return, but not with so much hustle and bustle. These processions start back from the tank where the image is immersed in water. One year the author saw the immersion ceremony at nine o'clock in the evening when it was raining heavily. It was on the *ghat* (bathing place) of a huge pucca tank—about one furlong in length and the same in width—that processions with gas lights came and handed over their images to a couple of men sitting in a tiny boat who immediately plied their oars and went right into the middle of the tank where, with a shout of praise to Ganpati, gently let the image slip into the water. This gondola-like boat carried one gas light which, in the pitch darkness and subdued hush of the people, produced a wonderfully beautiful effect. The boatmen would come for an image and go back with it audibly splashing the dark water of the tank with their tiny oars. Standing on the bank one could see in the background the oriental bazaar and the small processions of singing choirs emerging out of dark alleys, converging at the tank where in silence they would hand over the image in as gentle a manner as is handed over a funeral box to the party on the grave-side. People here looked like ghosts, moving about gently, in and out of the light, their wet clothing clinging to their bodies.

The day immediately after the festival is reserved by certain people for entertaining friends in a novel way. It is not commonly done as far as the author knows. But he knows it is done in the family of a Raja. In his drawing room there is a huge image of Ganpati who has a sort of elephantine smile of a self-complacent nature with a mischievous wink in one eye. He sits dressed up in English coat and waistcoat, the latter high enough, or opened in front in order to show his big and deep navel pit. He has a wrist watch too. The friends of the Raja sit in front of the image and eat and drink and make merry. Some one tries to shake his big belly and asks him as to what all it contains, another invites him to partake of something, the third puts a sweetmeat ball in his navel pit and makes some funny remark when all laugh, and Ganpati seems to smile too. They keep constantly joking and laughing at the expense of Ganpati who, of course, does not mind as one can see from his ever benevolent but impotent smile. Thus they spend hours in his jolly company. This day he is called Maskhara Ganpati—joker Ganpati.

TULSI VIVAHA

THE twelfth of Kartik is set apart for the wedding of the Tulsi plant to the God Vishnu who on this day wakes up from his four months' sleep. This plant, "Sweet Basil", whose Urdu name is 'Niyaz Bo' is quite common in India. Even the untouchable, who may not have a decent house to live in, gladly builds a raised pedestal of bricks to accommodate this plant, and he whitewashes and nicely decorates it with all sorts of sacred designs in different colours. If this plant happens to shoot out, even in an awkward part of the house, no Hindu will dare remove it, for it is sacred, being the wife of the great God Vishnu. It contains the spirit of a woman whom Vishnu loved. A woman by name Brinda was so lovely and pious that her husband could defy even the great God Shiva who could not kill him. Shiva referred the matter to his colleague Vishnu who could only lessen the power of the husband by dishonouring his wife. Her honour destroyed, and her husband killed, she burnt herself on the funeral pyre. But Vishnu had been struck by Cupid's arrow, and could not live without Brinda. So all the gods got together in a conference and decided to put the spirit of his beloved in a Tulsi plant in order to satisfy him. So this is how this plant has come to be regarded as sacred. Women worship this plant every evening at sunset, the time when the spirit is supposed to enter into it. Spirits are supposed to live in trees, or at least visible at night time and not in the day time.

From this day begins the marriage season of the Hindus which ends in the month of Asadh. For the Tulsi wedding, the same preparations are made that are made for human marriage. A fast is kept till the evening when the worship, or the wedding ceremony, begins. The image of Vishnu, generally of his incarnation Krishna, made of brass, or his picture (no clay image is used on this day) or a black stone called Salagram is placed by the side of the plant, and the material of worship placed in front. Pakwans or eatables prepared for marriage generally are Papar, Bhaje, Puri, Puranpoli, Sevai, Laddu, Dal, curry and vegetables. The things used as a 'sacrament' are Dhan ki Lahi—parched rice, Poha,—steamed rice and sugar, sugar drops—batasas, and also curd, ghee, milk and honey. Before the wedding ceremony the plant as well as the image is washed with water, and the material of worship is carefully arranged. A piece of cloth is hung between the image and the plant just as in actual marriage between the bride and the bridegroom. According to the instructions of the presiding priest who sits bathed and clad with white cloth (and ready for his fees, too), the headman of the family keeps throwing on the plant and the image the materials of worship, and the priest recites his mantras. The last mantra is called 'Mangal Ashtaka'. This is the mantra without which a marriage cannot take place. If all the mantras are recited except this, the marriage is supposed not to have taken place. The last word in this mantra is Savadhan, the literal meaning of which is "Be careful" which conveys the meaning "You are united now". This expression Savadhan is the most important word in the whole wedding ceremony, being the *sine qua non.* Once a boy who did not want to marry a particular girl ran away just before this word was pronounced and the marriage was supposed not to have taken place. Rice and red powder mixed together which is called *Akshada* is previously distributed to the friends and relatives assembled together, and at the time of reciting the word 'Savadhan' by the priest, when the cloth curtain is removed, all of them throw it on the plant and the image, and clap hands to show their approval. Immediately after that, in a brass plate, is placed a receptacle of kneaded flour, burning a cotton wick in clarified butter, and a little burning camphor, and red powder, etc., and waved before the bride and the bridegroom in a circular way from left to right for four or five times. The plant is touched with the image and the ceremony is over. It may be noted here that the cloth curtain is not hung at the time of Puja, it is only just before the 'Mangal Ashtaka' that the screen is placed and taken out after the saying of the 'Savadhan.' In the case of the marriage of man and woman, the latter keeps her face covered, and discards purdah after some time, though not so in North India, where women keep purdah and cover their faces. Just as on her wedding day the bride wears green-coloured bangles, so a few pairs of bangles of the same colour are put on the branches of the plant, and similarly a piece of good and new cloth is hung on the plant just like the bride on her wedding day. At the time of the actual wedding ceremony and worship, the bride and the bridegroom do not wear new clothes but old and dirty-looking ones, because water is thrown at them and are drenched through and through. So in actual marriage, the god is offered clothes and sandalwood paste and Jenauvara, the sacred thread, and the plant Kunku, Haldi—turmeric, and Mangal Sutar—the marriage necklace. In the marriage of man and woman, the woman is given by the husband a Mangal Sutar, *i.e.*, a necklace made of gold beads, and jorvey (toe rings); for at least on two toes she should have rings of silver. If these two things are not worn, the marriage cannot take place. Any woman with these two things can safely be said to be married as long as her husband is living. On becoming a widow she lias to take off these things. The green-coloured bangles are broken immediately after the husband's death. While in married life, and at the time of the wedding she marks her forehead with red powder; but in widowhood she cannot do so. The absence of these three things, at leat in the Central Provinces, and in the South, and also in the West of India, show that a particular Hindu woman is a widow. In some places and castes, such women shave their heads, and wear white clothes—a dress of mourning, as black is in the West. The widow wears no jewellery and is expected to take food which is not tasty, and quite separately. She is looked down upon by other members of her family. She is considered to have lost her husband on account of her sins in the past life, and in certain castes is not allowed to remarry.

There is no general rejoicing on the Tulsi wedding day such as is common on other festivals.

Tulsi is a common name among Hindu girls, and among men, such names as Tulsi Das, the servant of Tulsī.

DASEHRA

DURING this festival which lasts for nine days people take a gadwa or copper pot, and a wooden teapoy. In the middle of the table they draw a small circle within which they scatter rice mixed with gulal—red powder. In the centre of the circle is placed the gadwa, the neck of which is covered with mango leaves wrapped round and tied with a thread. A few leaves are placed vertically in the pot also which is previously filled with red rice.

Now in the midst of the big leaves is placed an image of Devi or goddess Kali, and with the help of mantras recited by the Brahmins, the worship goes on for nine days. The worship is conducted by a Brahmin every morning. This is called Ghattas thapna *i.e.*, the settlement or the well establishment or installation of the goddess in the house. On the tenth day occurs the Dasehra when Pakwans or delicious eatables (especially made for the occasion) are offered to the goddess—of course the Brahmins are the people who really eat them.

Now on this tenth day the goddess is taken out of the gadwa and placed in the usual place in the house. This day she is supposed to have gone to her abode and the people are happy because they had the honour of entertaining her.

The Rakshasas or demons having let themselves loose in the world the people through sheer helplessness prayed to Ashtbhuja Devi (the goddess with eight arms—Durga or Kali (mother) to protect them from their depredations; especially from Maheshasur, the baffalo demon, who was the worst of them all. It was on the tenth day that she destroyed the arch-demon, a symbol of the evil one, which was so easily destroyed and the world consequently made safe. This fact and the knowledge that it was no other than Kali or Durga herself who had killed it and given peace to the world adds to their enjoyment of the festival. It is for this reason that in almost every part of India, especially in places where the Dasehra is observed for the sake of Durga only that one finds that on this day a buffalo is sacrificed in front of the image of the goddess. The author has had many occasions of witnessing this sacrifice among the people of the Himalaya mountain, especially the Rajputs.

In some of the native states of the Himalayas, on Dasehra day, some elderly member of the ruling family performs the ceremony of severing the head off the body of the huge buffalo which is drugged for this occasion with bhang (Hemp) and country wine. It is brought in by means of strong ropes and kept in a position by a few men, in the midst of a huge crowd, all round, all eager to witness the performance of the ceremony. After going through the necessary worship the Prince gets ready with his drawn sword while the men untie the buffalo, who all this time has been looking all round with blood shot eyes, apparently painfully conscious of some impending disaster. As soon as the preparations are complete the prince strikes on the neck with tremendous force while a Gurkha soldier specially appointed behind the animal strikes on the hind legs in order to prevent him from running away very far from the place. The practice of striking at the legs was not resorted to in past years but on account of the sacrificial buffalo once having been instrumental in killing a few men by running amok among them after the stroke, such practice was discontinued and precautionary measures were adopted. In short, it was a queer sight to see the huge black thing running about for a minute or so with his neck hanging down with blood gushing out and his hind legs being almost severed by the Rajput soldier running behind him dealing stroke after stroke till the poor animal fell down exhausted, with helpless looks, begging for mercy. How he groaned! In a few minutes all was over, the death blows completely severing the head which was taken and placed before the image of Durga who never looks appeased; who wants to suck more blood and still more blood, sometimes longing for human blood also. She prefers it thousand times more to that of the buffalo and she does get it occasionally openly or secretly from her illiterate and superstitious followers who have implicit faith in her. It is said that in the remote corners of Assam such incidents do come to light every now and then. Until very recently the Khonds living round about northern Madras have been known to practice human sacrifice systematically.

The second time this sacrifice was observed by the author, was at the foot of the Siwalik Hills where in the courtyard of a romantic looking temple, shadowed by a huge *peepul*—Ficus religeosi tree, the same process was gone through but with the addition of scores of goats being killed with the help of the Gurkhas khukris severing the neck at one stroke with the sound of tch.

The glimpse at the life size image of Durga —as seen in a temple in the Punjab hills—standing in a somewhat dark room inspires one's heart with fear. As you step inside you find standing before you a jet black, weired looking, huge woman with dishevelled hair, having big, bloodshot, protruding eyes, and big, red tongue hanging out—a really fierce looking thing—with eight long hands, each one holding something, especially the two hands;

holding in one of the right hands a dagger besmeared with fresh blood as if it had just cut the human head which is shown held in one of her left hands. People shout "Kali Mata (Kali mother) ki jai." They rend the very sky with their shouts in her praises. But why not. Is she not Kali the Terrible, Kali the Revenger, the omnipotent mother of the world who stands no nonsense, who commands the homage of the world; the goddess who creates havoc if not obeyed, if not worshipped, if not appeased by the freshest blood, yea, even of human beings.

In Bengal Durga Puja holds exclusive sway over the people. The ten days are entirely devoted to the worship of the goddess alone; the tenth day being the special day for her.

Durga Puja in Bengal should really take place in spring but on account of the goddess's helping Ram in rescuing his wife from the clutches of Rawan in the autumn season, it is not observed in the former. The story is that Ram in spite of his great millitary skill found himself absolutely powerless against Rawan who seemed to be a weak enemy. He thought in his mind that there must be someone bigger and stronger than Rawan who was guarding him. Through the spies sent in all directions for the investigation of this matter it was discovered that Rawan was being protected by a hidden power. It was Durga Now according to Durga's own "religious" principles no one could invoke her blessing or solicit her attention unless she was worshipped with the help of 108 lotus flowers. Ram's constant companion, the monkey god, Hanuman, went all over the world—an easy affair for him—and secured the desired number of blue lotuses. Now when Durga saw this, she felt greatly dismayed as she had then to leave Rawan and transfer her favours to Ram. But she played a trick on Ram. She stole one flower out of the lot, thus rendering the worship impossible. But Ram was not to be discouraged. He immediately lifted his arrow to take out his own eye to substitute for the wanting lotus. When Durga saw this, she immediately replaced the lotus and thus Ram was able to complete his worship. No sooner had it been done than Ram got the power to overcome Rawan. Now this worship by Ram was done in autumn hence the reason for Durga Puja being observed in this season.

Bengal is the only place where Durga Puja is conducted with so much pomp and show. It is as important for Bengal Hindus as Christmas is for Christians. Long vacation is given in schools and colleges. Children are given a good time. In a place like Calcutta shopping is done vigorously. Many on this day spend lavishly their income of months. New clothes and new things are presented to the young wives both by parents and husbands.

The image of Durga as seen in Bengal is as follows:—She looks like a woman full of wrath; has ten hands, each holding a discus, a sword, a trident, a lance, an arrow, a bow, a shield, a goad, a noose and an axe. She has three eyes, one being in the forehead. She has in front of her a lion, a demon and a buffalo. On her left and right are Saraswati and Lukshmi. In the right corner sits Ganpati, the elephant god and on the left sits another god who is supposed to grant favours to the worshippers.

On Daserah day which is the tenth day, the image of this goddess is taken to the river in procession with great pomp and show, and there immersed in water.

People who are ignorant of the significance of Durga worship generally regard this goddess as cruel and a being who is appeased by blood—say of goats and buffaloes as is the common practice all over India; and for that matter, human lives also have been sacrificed at her shrine. But people who know, say that the goddess wants these animals not for their own sakes but as representations and embodiment of the evil passions of human beings. This goddess should be a purifying agency, suggesting repentence from past sins, but it seems that people have almost wholly ignored this side of the sacrifice and have taken to the easy method of buying a goat from bazaar and cutting it in front of the image thereby feeling satisfied that the goddess wanted toll and that has been given. After the Puja is finished, they go home in the happy thought that she would not be merciless during the year. How cheap yet in certain cases, at what a high cost. At her shrine fathers have sacrificed their daughters and mothers their sons, brothers their sisters and sisters their brothers. Numerous children have been stolen to be sacrificed thus and many culprits have been brought to book. Human sacrifice has not been uncommon in India though it is no longer so. But in out of the way corner, away in the jungles of India every now and then comes a reminder to say that such sacrifices are still done to a certain extent. But in the minds of millions of ignorant Hindus the belief is ingrained that gods do want human sacrifice. They cannot get over it. Buffaloes and goats are of course substitutes for direct human sacrifice but then there is another kind of sacrifice also. It is not an uncommon practice for old men and women to leave their homes and pass the rest of their lives on meagre and unwholesome food in places of pilgrimage so that by dying in such places they may attain speedy salvation and immediate bliss of heaven. Even now, in the big fairs held in places like Hardwar, Allahabad and Benares, situated on the banks of the sacred river Ganges, sometimes scores of lives are lost in the rush of religious frenzy, and occasionally one can see dead bodies floating in the river.

Almost every river, lake, tank and well is reputed to take its annual bhent—a toll of human sacrifice. The common belief is that the gods residing in them must have sacrifices of human beings, and therefore every year at least one human being should die by being drowned in each river, lake or tank. When thousands and hundreds of thousands of people take their bath in them in a year, it is quite likely for at least one person out of so many to be the victim of an accident. Superstitious as the uneducated Hindus are, they take such accidental deaths as sacrifices demanded by the gods residing in the river or lake or tank. Similarly a new bridge on a river or a dam requires, in their opinion, the sacrifice of at least one or two children before the god will allow it to be constructed. During the process of building, mothers do not allow their children to wander for fear of their being caught by Government agents for sacrifice to the god or goddess of the spot concerned!

This deep seated idea of the propitiation of human beings for the gods is not confined to the rivers or lakes only. In the Deccan (South) there exists a common semi-religious belief that every treasure trove is jealously guarded by a spirit which in order to deliver it up demands human sacrifice. So in order to procure a child for that purpose, neighbours' children prove quite handy. It was only recently that a rich widow caught hold of a child of one year of age and buried it alive and put an oil lamp on its head. Occasionally such incidents happen in many parts of India. The practice of human sacrifice is resorted to not only to gain a certain end but it seems that it might be used for any purpose for which a person considers it a speedy remedy. For instance, in a small town a Hindu woman who was childless and was anxious to have one of her own, caught hold of a beautiful boy of 12 through the help of a chamar (a leather worker—a low caste) who slaughtered the boy in the woman's house. As the blood gushed out fresh and warm she took a bath in it–naked in the light of an oil lamp. The idea was to appease the god or goddess (of what)? to grant her the capacity to conceive, and most curiously, she did conceive. Thus instances where human sacrifice is resorted to can be multiplied. The custom of human sacrifice to appease the local deity is being controlled by Government among the aborigines living in the mountains of India. A few years ago, in a backward town in the Central Provinces a woman killed two young children in a most violent manner in the presence and with the consent of their father. The father looked on this gruesome process of killing without protest, the reason being that the woman had declared herself the temporary incarnation of mother Kali or Durga in her mood of destruction. She said that she was being urged to do this deed by a voice from within. So the father in his great horror was helpless when he realized that none other than goddess Kali herself was concerned in the matter. No one dare cross her path. The woman was tried in a court of law and was declared guilty by the judge.

Let us now after a long digression revert to the subject of the observance of Dasehra. In the plains of the Punjab, especially in the interior and on the north west the victory of Ram over Ravan is in fact the only incident which is celebrated with impresive ceremonies particularly by the burning of the effigy of Ravan, the king of Ceylon. As observed in one of the cities, a party of about twenty or thirty men dress up in posteens—fur coats—with the inner part turned out and head also covered up with a hairy cover, all giving the appearance of a black and brown bear standing on his hind legs. The waist is covered with crude copper bells, generally used for cattle, which produce fearful noise. These men disguised in such awe-inspiring and gruesome dress emerge from different lanes and bylanes of the city and rush towards an appointed place in the main street from where perspiring and sweating, making an awful noise with their bells, with bows and arrows in their hands they run at top speed towards the spot on which the effigy of Rawan is to be burnt. These men who represent the Rakshasas or demons, the soldiers of Ravan, go and dance about Rawan putting up a great show of fighting with arrows until to their great dismay, Maruti or Hanuman, the monkey god, takes a handful of long dry grass especially provided for the purpose and with it sets fire to the effigy. The effigy is prepared every year, a day or two before Dasehra. It is sometimes about 80 ft. high erected on a huge frame-work of bamboos. The frame-work of course is all covered up with layers upon layers of thick papers dyed all red except certain portions which are dyed pale blue and yellow to distinguish the collars of the red mantle and button holes etc. The whole structure from top to bottom is like a barrel. On the upper end of the barrel structure ten big grim human faces were embossed all around and from the middle of the barrel came out a long thick neck on which was set most proportionately the head and face of a donkey of jet black colour having black human eyes, set in white eye balls. Rawan was a Rakshas with ten faces. From the shoulders projected two long arms holding a bow and an arrow ready to shoot. The effigy of another demon half the size of Rawan was also seen standing beside him. The inside of Rawan is filled up with bombs, squibs and crackers, and to one not near enough to witness the scene the noise and the conflagation would appear more like that of a battle than a homely burning of an effigy. As the effigy of Rawan burns, the thousands of people who stand around, shout 'Ramchander ki jai', thus commemorating the victory of Raja Ramchander. In this particular city a Palki having a handsome boy dressed as a woman representing Sita, the wife of Ramchander, is also carried about the streets following musical bands, in memory of the release of the queen from the clutches of a demon king. Palki is a sort of wooden palanquin with a golden facade having a niche and a seat in it for Sita to sit on. The whole thing is mounted on a wooden platform dragged on small wheels. Facade is all golden, made with golden paper pasted all over with golden edges and frills, having been decorated with bright purple and dark blue bulbs.

One feature observed in the Dasehra fair was that of a few non-Hindus bringing, in covered cages, birds called Nilkanth—blue jays. This bird is much sought after this day as the people do not have their dinners that evening until they see it. They keep looking about for it all the time. These people charge special fees to allow individuals to have a look on them and if they press them to liberate the birds they expect handsome compensation for each one. For this purpose therefore they have more than one bird in stock. Hindus consider this a bird of good omen. Nilkanth is one of the names of the god Shiva also.

The Dasehra of Kullu in the Punjab is considered to be remarkable in many respects, in spite of its being situated in an out of the way place. Hundreds of thousands of people congregate on the big plain of Dhalpur from all over the Province, particularly to do business in woollen goods, horses, honey, tea and fruits. About four hundred gods dance with the hill people, and the invariably fair and beautiful women of Kullu Valley, clad in queer costumes and covered with silver ornaments of all kinds, spend their entire time in listening to the music and watching the dances of different groups. These hill people are simple and remarkably free in social life. Among them one might forget that one is in India. Except for three months in a year, these people spend their time in drinking, dancing and attending fairs.

However, besides burning the effigy of Rawan, in some towns the career of Raja Ramchander is also recited to the Hindus during the ten days of Dasehra. It is called Ram Lila, the story of Rama. When the shops are closed and quiet reigns in bazars and the evening meal is over, people begin pouring in the courtyard of the biggest temple of the town at about 9 o'clock. While men take off their shoes and sit down on big durries, women go to a side door and go up the stairs to the roofs adjoining all round the courtyard, and sit down on the edge with their faces half covered. At about 10 o'clock the Brahmin sits down at the raised seat with an Indian harmonium by his side if he knows how to play at it, otherwise sits with legs crosswise and a garland round his neck and a mark of sandalwood paste, or red or yellow rice stuck on his forehead. He has in front of him a big thick vernacular book, the Ramayan from which he reads a few shlokes (verses) in a thundering but singsong manner and then translates it in simple Hindustani which he expresses in a special tone—the melodius tone with its soft and graded cadences.

After singing a few shlokes he would begin translating the same in Hindustani with all proper emphasis and would go on for some time till for climactic purposes he, followed by the congregation would punctuate the Katha (this religious recitation) with shouts of "Bolo, Raja Ramchander ki jai" (say, Raja Ramchander be praised), with exaggerated emphasis on the last word. The story lasts for a number of nights always. The last night is a profitable one for the reciter, for on this night he is given presents for his labour. Money is previously subscribed for the purpose. He may be given a Kashmere blue shawl, a shoulder cloth, a turban and some batasas or sweets etc. And he surely deserves it.

The other method is to act his life, especially the part connected with his exile. The show as observed by the author once in a hill town of the Punjab would give one an idea of the miracle plays of the Middle Ages.

Another reason for holding this day as a sacred day is that on this day i.e., Dasehra, Panduas went to the Shami tree—Malabathricum—after fourteen (thirteen?) years to get back their weapons which they had deposited in the care of the tree itself; especially by Arjun whose other name is Vijaya—Victorious—one of the five Panduas who defeated Karus. Pandus had been ordered Banbas (to live in forest—in exile) by Daryodhan of Karus, who was the prince (veritable King), son of Dhritrashtra, king of Karus. The fight took place after this banbas. In some places this day is called the warrior's Day.

In Indian Native-States this day is reserved for inspection by the Maharaja of all the weapons of war—guns, spears, swords, canons, daggers and shields and ammunition, etc., besides all other necessary articles stored in the Toshakhana (the store) such as tents, Howdahs, etc., the idea being to be quite ready in case war should break out or the Maharaja himself might decide to attack a neighbouring king. Dasehra comes off immediately after the rains and in olden times the kings actually started their wars from this day, being auspicious and considered as the day of victory. The nullahs, the rivers and streams would be dry for the army to cross over, and the weather cool and pleasant, and longer marches could be effected. Though these days the possibilities of war with the neighbouring states are remote being under British suzerainty, yet the Maharaja at the head of a big procession of elephants and horses fully prepared for war, starts with his State forces and guns, and passing through the streets goes out to the outskirts of the city accompanied by a musical band and returns after dark the same evening. This custom is not confined to the Hindu Rajas only but has become a tradition in some of the Mohamedan States also, where if the Commander-in-Chief is Hindu, he goes out at the head of his forces, otherwise any Hindu Minister of the state would do. It must be remembered that before the weapons are taken out, the Maharaja worships them with the help of the Brahmin of the palace. This custom of worshipping the weapons is considered so auspicious that the non-warrior classes also have taken it up to suit their own purposes. It is curious that on this day soldiers worship their weapons, Banyas (Vaishyas shopkeepers) their weighing scales and weights, goldsmith the implements of his art, farmer his ploughs, etc., and grainseller his wooden or iron pailees (a measuring basin) and so on. They worship the same in the belief that thereby they would be blessed more. All such implements are washed in water, in milk and then nicely arranged in front of the usual seat where these are worshipped with the usual material of worship—Rice, sandalwood paste, red powder and flowers, etc. This worship is conducted in the forenoon without the help of a Brahmin.

During Mahratta reign the Peshwas used to go out with all eclat on this day and stay outside the city from where they could actually start on expeditions and start campaigns in earnest. They could then stay out for eight months and be back for the rainy season; that is for Asardh, Shravan, Bhadrapad and Aswin. Now the custom among the people is that a few men are sent outside the city in the morning to get a branch of Apta tree—B. Racemosa and plant it somewhere there in the open. The leaves of this tree are oval in shape and joined together. In the evening, parties of friends and relatives go to the place along with a sword with which the planted branches are wounded, the leaves so fallen are gathered together, in fact, there takes place a great struggle over them and the fun is enjoyed by all, like young children looting fruits under a tree. The leaves are brought to the city where they are distributed as greetings of love to friends and relatives and also to old people who themselves are not strong enough to go on such expeditions and who because of their age have to stay at home. After handing over the leaves to the old folk they touch their feet and then fold their hands in reverence and wish them long life and happiness and in response the old people bless them most profusely. Such leaves are freely exchanged among friends as greetings for Dasehra.

The author has once observed a Raja of an old family (but no more ruling) going out this day with his elephants, camels and horses to an appointed place outside the city and wounding with his sword his special Shami tree the leaves of which are gathered by him and his friends and strangers also. Raja himself enjoys the fun thoroughly. While some go to pick up the leaves, others go to see the face of the Raja, for it is considered highly auspicious to do so on this day. In those places where Rajas can't be seen people wait for nilkanth—blue jay—which is regarded in the same light, it having the same blue stripe across its neck as the great God Shiva had in conse quence of drinking by mistake the poison which had most luckily not gone down beyond the Adam's apple before he discovered the mistake. The poison was so strong that it left an indelible mark on the throat. If the god had died in consequence of it one can hardly imagine what would have happened to the world!

Those who are men of means present their mother, father, brothers and sisters real gold either in the shape of ornaments or in lumps; the idea is that Ram after killing Rawan had looted Lanka and brought back a large quantity of gold for distribution among relatives and friends. His soldiers must have done the same thing.

This day is called seemolanghan also which

means 'the crossing of the boundary, or the crossing of the boundaries of the kingdom': the reason being as mentioned above, that in former days, kings used to embark on fresh expeditions on this day because of its being a very auspicious one, and if there was no battle to be fought, they would at least take out their troops and pitch the tents, outside the city. The above was one way of observing the custom, the one mentioned below is a bit different. In the evening after four o'clock a very large number of men (excluding women of course) actually start on some expedition (imaginary and sometimes real also) and cross the boundary, that is, they go out of the city to a considerable distance in order to cross the boundary or the outskirts of the city. They go shouting, yelling, talking and laughing, carefree and happy and assemble under a Shami tree the leaves of which they pluck and carry home as precious as pieces of gold. On reaching their homes they wait outside the doors—in fact the ladies of the house are already waiting at the door. They are ready with milk and water and as the men step in, the sisters, the mothers the wives and other female relatives turn by turn pour milk and water on the feet of the men, the idea being to cleanse them and free them from foul things—physically and spiritually. The men are supposed to have returned victorious from war. The pouring of milk and water is considered as a mark of great respect to them.

As soon as the ceremony of the washing of feet is finished, the ladies apply gulal—red powder—to men's fore-heads, throw rice on their heads and then receive them inside the house. The red powder and rice are brought in a brass plate in which a lamp of kneaded flour containing clarified butter or ghee and a cotton rolled-up wick which is kept burning during the worship, is also placed. No Brahmin is required for this purpose. After the ceremony is over they go out in their neighbourhood to their relatives and friends' houses to distribute the leaves they plucked from the tree. In fact, they hand over the leaves to any one they meet on the road, acquaintance or otherwise, and they do it with great joy too. The leaves are given out as veritable gold. Immediately after exchanging them the two embrace each other warmly whether friend or foe (?) signifying that they forgive each other's past offences.

There is yet another reason given by some people for the celebrating of the tenth of Ashwin and that is that this day has been fixed for merry-making in anticipation of ripening of crops after the rains. Their belief is that after the rains the prospects of the crops should be good and expectations of a good harvest great. Farmers consequently have ample time at their hands to indulge in any pastime they like as they do not have to sow or harvest their crops.

In some of the towns of Mahrashtra the Dasehra is observed in memory of the great Marhatta warrior Shivaji also.

By some Hindus, three and a half days in a year are considered very auspicious and one of them is Dasehra. The days are Dasehra, Divali (Bali pratipada), Ganesh-Chaturti, and half a day of Nag-Panchmi—the forenoon and not the afternoon. A new undertaking in order to be lucky and successful one must begin on one of these days. So if one observed carefully one would notice that new shops are opened this day, new business started, new public library opened or anything new is done on this day. Even children commence their school carrier on this day or on any of the other auspicious days.

DIVALI

(Bali Pratipada or the Feast of Lamps).

THE Divali festival, which is believed to date so far back as *Satya Yuga* (the age of Truth), takes place at the beginning of the month of Kartika, and is held in honour of Lakshmi, the Goddess of Wealth; or, to be more correct, it begins on the 13th of the dark half of *Aswin* and continues up to the second light half of *Kartik*.

As the name suggests, it is the feast of lamps. It is called Dipvali also; Deep = lamp, Vali = line; the line of lamps. Its other name is Dip-Malika or Dip-Mala, the String of Lamps.

The 'thirteenth day of the dark half' is the first day of tbe festival. People rise early, bathe and prepare for the occasion. Tho womenfolk begin scrubbing the cooking utensils. and sweeping the house; on that day everything in the house should be clean and tidy. After finishing all the sweeping and tidying up the house, they sit down to prepare *Pakwans* (special eatables); and while the women are busy at home, the men are engaged in sweeping their shops. On that day all the streets in the town are very dirty, on account of the rubbish thrown away by the shopkeepers and it is a heavy job for the Municipal sweepers to sweep from one end of the town to the other.

All the white-washing is finished by this day, and in some towns about 95 per cent of the houses are white-washed, while those who cannot afford to do this, plaster their houses with fine earth.

Special signs such as the Svastika (a cross mark' which is Lakshmi's emblem and also that of Vishnu and Shiva) and stars are marked on the front doors and courtyards. All sorts of designs are drawn. Tin pots perforated with different designs, such as a man riding on a bicyle or on horse back, or different kinds of flowers, are filled with powdered chalk. and are 'struck' on the wetted ground, thus leaving the white designs conspicuous on a darkish ground. The whole of the courtyard of the front of the house is thus decorated. A few days before the festival the shopkeepers begin to bring out their stock of pictures for sale, as these are in great demand for decorating the interior of the houses.

Chinese and Japanese lamps and locally-made hexagonal lamps and coloured papers are also in great demand, as the meaning of the word Divali is the feast of lamps, when the whole town is illuminated. The hexagonal lamps are generally suspended from the ends of long bamboos as high as possible and for the whole month of Kartik; the idea being to guide in their journey the gods and sages who have since become planets.

This day the shopkeepers and other business-men close the year's accounts, and open new accounts. According to Samvat Era, instituted by King Vikramajit, Divali is the new year of the mercantile people. Our 1932 is their 1989. According to Saka Era 1932 is equivalent to 1854. The first of the first-month of the Hindus, *i.e.* Chaitra, is the new year day commonly observed by the people. All the books are brought out and placed in a heap. Gold and silver are also brought out and put along with the books. The man worships them with Haldi and Sandur (turmeric and red powder). The gold and silver money is washed in milk and kept in front in a heap sprinkled over with powdered turmeric and red powder—traces of such powder can often be found on rupees which are in circulation after the festival. After finishing with this they worship Lakshmi (the Goddess of Wealth). Some take a basket and fill it with grains and keep it in the middle of the room covered with a piece of cloth and sprinkled over with flowers. The family members sit round it and await the arrival of Lakshmi. They sit thus the whole night, and keep their eyes fixed on the basket, in order to be sure to see Lakshmi come. She does come, invisible to the eyes, but if she is not watched for, her sister Alakshmi—the Goddess of Misfortune—might creep in in her place. So they have to be very careful!

This day is considered to be a very auspicious day. Whenever people want to start on new things, they postpone them to this day. Children are sent to school on this day. Mothers send their newly married daughters to their husbands' homes on this day, in the hope of the daughter getting a child, or saving her from being harshly treated by her husband. Goldsmiths get any amount of orders this day. It is in fact the merchants' 'new year day'. Some clever business-men issue special 'Divali cards' silvery letters, printed with on one side with the wording of the invitation asking the pleasure of your company at a pansupari or 'social gathering'; which means that you go into the well-decorated shop, sit down on a chair; the manager or the merchant comes up to you smiling, offers you a pan packet, a garland, a nosegay, and rubs some perfumed ointment on the back of your hands. You bow and you are off; thus people keep coming in and going out. You go to another shop and yet another and so on till you feel that you are feeling giddy with overfeeding yourself with pans and overloading yourself with garlands.

Kora cloth (new cloth which has never been washed or used before) is worn this day. The shops of the sellers of bronze and brass vessels are specially decorated and illuminated; this is because a new utensil bought on this day and used then for the first time is very auspicious. New utensils previously bought are kept unused until Divali. Anything borrowed before the festival is returned this day, especially money!

The second day is celebrated for showing gratitude to the God Krishna, who killed Narakasura on this day. Narakasura was a demon who had greatly troubled the people. Krishna killed him, thus restoring happiness in the world. This day is called *Narak Chaturdashi* (*Chatur* = 4, *Dashi* = 10 = 14th).

The third day is *Amavasia* (Full dark night) reserved for Lakshmi Puja or the worship of the Goddess of Wealth. She is worshipped in the evening, along with other gods, with the nessary materials of worship—sweetmeats, milk, flowers, etc. This is followed by a grand feast, very much relished and enjoyed after the day's fast.

The fourth day is for Bali-pratipada. Bali, a demon, was so generous that he excelled all, even the gods, in merit. He was considered to be a great danger for the well-being of the people, because of his excessive generosity. He naturally excited the jealousy of all the gods. They were afraid lest he should grow too powerful by his meritorious deeds. Vishnu undertook to punish Bali for his boldness, and took the incarnation of Vaman. (Vaman = a dwarf, a pigmy = a deceiver.) This Brahman dwarf came to Bali and requested a boon in charity, the boon being the grant of as much ground as he could measure with his three steps. Poor Bali did not know that the disguised Brahman dwarf was none other than Vishnu himself and that he would cover the three worlds in those three steps of his. Bali granted the boon, not knowing the consequences. This dwarf grew into a tremendous size and measured this world with one of his feet, his next measure was the upper world, and his third step was on the head of Bali pushing him down to *Patal* or the nether world where he eventually made him the king to rule over the dead. Thus the fourth day is celebrated in memory of the pushing down of Bali to the nether world, thus giving "peace" to the world. But Bali, the king of the nether world, was so very very generous that even Vishnu agreed to be the watchman at his gate!

On this day women make an image of 'Bali Raja' out of cowdung and keep it in the courtyard where they worship it with the usual material of worship. After worship they sweep and collect all the rubbish of the house in a basket, and upon that rubbish keep a light, a pice and a broom. They hand it over to a servant who is followed by one of the children of the house. The boy keeps on striking a bronze plate as he follows, and goes on reciting loudly the following. "Let all sorts of miseries perish and the kingdom of Bali Raja come back again!" With accompaniment of this recitation the servant throws away the rubbish on the refuse heap, meaning thereby that by so doing all the miseries shall be thrown away.

The fifth day is *Yamadvitya* (= second day for Yama). This fifth day is also called *Bhaubij.* On this day Yama, the God of Death went on a visit to Agra, to see his sister Yamuna. (The River Jamna passes through Agra). Another version is that the moon also went to his sister on this day. He was received with great eclat and hospitality. This tradition gave rise to the custom of brothers visiting their sisters on this day. Sisters (married sisters) invite their brothers to their houses and welcome them with feasts etc., and expect to receive from them in return money or ornaments, sarees or any other thing which brothers think their sisters would cherish most.

The brother arrives at his sister's house early in the morning and takes off all his clothes except the loin cloth preparatory to taking a bath. The sister anoints his body with scented oils which is followed by 'ubtan'. This is a yellow cream made of turmeric and perfumes. Then she pours warm water on him and he bathes. All the time this pretty ceremony is going on, the musical band stationed near by keeps playing some Indian tunes. In the case of a Raja it is suplemented by the firing of guns also. The rocket-bombs and other fire-works are freely used to celebrate the occasion, both by the rich and the poor. After the bath if the sister is younger than her brother she does obeisance to him by touching his feet and doing *namaskar* with folded hands; *vice versa* if the sister is older than her brother. The mother can perform this ceremony if a man has no sister. Ordinarily in such a case the wife of the man's best friend anoints his body and gives the bath. A friend's wife can perform this ceremony even if he has a sister but lives far away from the town in which he is living and is unable to take the long journey. The man's own wife is not expected to give such a bath to her husband. The breakfast taken at noon this day should have been prepared by the person who has given the bath and none other.

The same evening as the moon rises, the sisters go out and have a look at the moon and then go into their houses and worship their brothers. On a brass plate is arranged rice (coloured or uncoloured), the red powder, one nut and a lamp made of kneaded flour, in which clarified butter and not oil is burnt. The brother takes the nut off the plate and keeps it till after the end of the worship when he presents it to his sister in return for her trouble or honour done to him; and it is after this that he offers money or ornaments or sarees, etc. She applies red powder on his forehead and then waves the plate containing the light in front of his body. She then throws rice on his head wishing him thereby prosperity and long life.

Worship finished, the whole family and guests, if invited, sit down to a sumptuous meal; the women, of course, take it after the men have finished. Children enjoy the special eatables tremendously. In fact, for children in India, as all over the world, these festivals don't mean anything but a sort of *tamasha*. They put on new suits, eat special *pakwans* and use plenty of rockets and squibs.

People undertake long railway journeys in order to be honoured by their sisters. A Brahmin once told me that he, being the only brother, had to go to his sister on every such occasion in order to please her, as his absence would mean a sort of mourning in his sister's house.

Those who have not been able to observe Divali on the fourth day, on account of death in the family, observe it on the fifth.

On two nights of the Divali, people freely and fully indulge in gambling; this being taken to be a religious affair, the Government does not enforce the law against it. The consequence is that in the public places or in the homes, both children and adults gamble to their hearts' content. It is commonly believed that this deplorable vice of gambling which has been the ruin of many has been enjoined by the Shastras. This is not correct. The *Rig-Veda* on the contrary says most definitely, that gambling should never be indulged in. Yet nobody appears to have made any serious effort to create a public opinion among Hindus against it; as can be noticed by any one who makes it a point to test this by visiting the bazaars and private houses during the Divali festival. Suspension of the law against gambling by the Government is itself a proof of Hindus taking it a part of the religion. Both the rich and the poor indulge in gambling these days in order to satisfy themselves religiously.

There are very many different ways and methods of gambling in the Indian bazaars; in fact one can gamble with anything in the world. The author has seen grown-ups playing generally with playing cards or on wooden boards marked with a circle and numbers, fitted with an iron needle to go round like a clock's. In many cities he has seen such stalls arranged at every few yards in a bazaar, each having a cluster of men round it. Another way is speculation, which requires no elaboration. Boys besides gambling in one of the manners given above, play also with pice thrown on a long map of many rectangles, or with walnuts, glass bullets or pice thrown into a small hole dug in the ground, or with pieces of slate pencils or kauri shells, in which case the players take each other's pencils or kauries out of a circle drawn on the ground; or by playing 'odd and even'.

Once the author saw a clever young man earning money for nothing. He had an earthenware flask with a long and narrow neck buried under the ground upto its mouth. On the mouth he kept, in a vertical manner, a stick made out of dirty rags, its length being a little over six inches and thickness about one and a half inches. He would ask one of the people gathered round him to put a pice on the top of it. To such a one he would hand over a wooden stick, with instructions to hit the cloth stick with it. In ninety-five cases out of a hundred, the cloth stick would be knocked away to a distance, but the pice would drop down into the flask. It was a condition that if the pice did *not* drop into the flask by so hitting the cloth stick, the owner of the flask would pay to the other man four times the amount. The man earned a lot by fooling so many people.

Why people gamble during Divali, few know. The author has inquired this of many Brahmins but not one contended that it is so enjoined by their Vedas. They say people just gamble for the sake of fun. Perhaps, this being the mercantile new year when balance sheets are prepared and profit and loss counted, people originally indulged in it, either for the sake of fun as a result of true prosperity, or to show off prosperity for the sake of their business. Both the rich and the poor, after counting their profit and loss, wanted respectively either to add more through avarice and greed or to make some profit as a last recourse.

As for social life in general during these days, youngsters have sweets to eat and squibs to let off; friends exchange sweets and fruits; business-men send gifts of sweets to their customers. "Toys" of sugar moulded into all sorts of animals and birds are the sweets peculiar to this festival. Sweetshops are full of them. *Kheel and *Batasas must be eaten by every Hindu on this day at least in the Punjab; they are eaten together. Well-lit shops display baskets full of this stuff.

For non-Hindus the only fun worth enjoying is of passing through the bazaars to see the houses and other buildings gorgeously and tastefully decorated, with thousands upon thousands of earthenware lamps arranged all over the roofs, doors, windows, cornices; on frames of bamboos erected for the purpose, arranged into letters of

---

*Kheel=Rice parched in hot sand, opens out like white flowers.

*Batasa or Patasa=Dried drops of sugar froth made by boiling sugar and dropping them on cloth.

welcome and others, sometimes on pinnacles of temples, even on perches of pigeons, erected on very high bamboo poles,—lamps so placed look very much like stars. Bankers and traders spend more than others in decorating their buildings. The shops of the sellers of bronze and brass utensils are worth seeing. People on this day keep lamps on wells, stores, warehouses and in the fields also, to keep away evil spirits and demons.

This night every Hindu lights as many earthenware lamps as his means allow. This is an index of the prosperity or otherwise of a house or a firm. There is a great rivalry and emulation to be noticed that evening. In cities which have electric power, people, who can afford it, cover the front part of their houses with hundreds of bulbs, which when reflected in the water of a tank nearby produce a most wonderful effect. The well-to-do use all shades and shapes of Chinese and Japanese paper-lamps, but in humbler homes, sexagonal and octagonal paper-lamps (Fanus) shed splendour in abundance. In the Punjab, especially in the North-West, one may notice huge drum-like white paper-lamps installed at short distances on the road and in the shops on which are visible facsimiles of all sorts of pictures moving round and round. Near the bottom of the white-paper drum there is a big hole through which an earthenware lamp containing mustard oil, with rolled up cotton wick, is burnt, put in and kept in the centre of the "drum". A little higher up from the bottom there is a middle pole to which are attached by means of spokes three 'circles' of bamboo twigs held apart at distances of one foot each, more or less, depending on the size of the lamp. Round the twigs are pasted different kinds of funny facsimiles, and as these revolve (they are pushed by hand) they throw their shadows on the white paper of the 'drum'. Both young and old cluster round and watch this with keen interest.

In the Punjab the best place to see Divali is Amritsar. The Durbar Sahib of Amritsar—the Golden Temple of the Sikhs—is a sight worth any trouble to see and people undertake long journeys to see it. The 'rush' during the 'Lamp Night' is so great that the Municipality has to issue passes and tickets for admission to go in to see the beautifully lit Golden Temple. It is surrounded by water on all sides, except for a streak of marble road which links it with the marble paths surrounding the tank. Behind it stands the Baba-Tal—the high tower—making the scene still more romantic.

As to the origin of the custom of lighting lamps on this evening, nobody seems to know for sure. Different origins are given, and are ascribed to different reasons. The following story shows at least one of the origins of the illumination of houses during Divali:—Vikramajit, king of Ujjain, in whose court Kalidas, the writer of "Shakuntala". was one of the nine gems—fell into hard times, in consequence of having incurred the ire of the powerful planet, Saturn. It came about this way. After Vikramjit had heard of the other eight planets, one of the 'nine gems' related the story of Saturn or Sani, and said how the Sun, his father, was eclipsed at the time of his birth. On hearing this, the king laughed and remarked "What sort of a son is this, who has brought disgrace to his father by his birth!" Saturn was greatly infuriated by the remark and came down to the earth in the form of a Brahmin, and went to the palace of the king with a swift running horse, with the apparent object of selling it. The king was informed, and immediately came out to try the horse. The Brahmin advised him to go towards the jungle. He had not gone far when the horse took him up in the air and alighted somewhere on the bank of a river in thick jungle, where he wandered about for days together. At last he reached a city. While he was still on the outskirts of it he met a shopkeeper who seeing he was such a handsome man, though not recognizing in him a king, thought of marrying his daughter to him and took him home. At night he made him asleep in the 'sitting room', or Baithak. After some time the shopkeeper instructed his daughter to go into the room. She went in and worshipped the man. On account of

Saturn's mischief the man would not wake up! However. she hung her precious pearl necklace on the peg and laid herself down with the man. After some time Vikramajit saw that a swan was eating away the pearls of the necklace one by one, yet he had not the power to prevent it from doing so. In the morning she demanded her necklace which he could not produce. Consequently the man was dragged up to the king (this kingdom was hundreds of miles away from Vikramajit's own kingdom) who after hearing both sides ordered his men to cut off the hands and legs of the man and to throw him outside the city walls, without providing him with any food. He lay there for six months, people supplying him with food out of pity. One day, a young bride who was on her way to her husdand's home in the territory of Vikramajit, happened to see this helpless man lying outside the city walls uncared for. She took pity on him and went back to the city and submitted an application to the king for permission to take the man along to Vikramajit's capital. This granted she arranged to carry the man. On reaching her destination she appointed him to mind the Ghan,* she being an oil-woman. One day he sang a *dip raga* (dip = lamp). By virtue

---

*Ghan—the big pestle used for grinding oil-seeds. It is run like the Persian wheel, pulled by oxen. It has a seat on one end of the beam, behind the ox, for the driver to sit upon. He was employed as a driver.

of this tune or raga, all the lamps of the city were lit by themselves! Now the daughter of the king who had punished Vikramajit happened to come to the palace of Vikramajit, to pay a visit of courtesy. On seeing the city so profusely lit up, remarked that there being no festival why the lamps of the city should be lit up. Immediately she sent servants to enquire if someone was singing *dip raga.* After an exhaustive enquiry it was found that a limbless man was singing the raga in the house of an oil-woman. He was brought into the presence of the princess who ordered him to sing the song again. On hearing it she fell in love with him, but she could not accept or marry him because he had no hands or legs. Vikramajit who of course knew his palace very well thought of his good old days and began to pray to God for mercy in order that either his limbs might be restored, or his life taken. The result of the prayer was the restoration of limbs and of his kingdom.

We are not sure whether this day led to Divali illumination or Divali fell on this day. It is popularly believed that the illumination is done in order to welcome the Goddess Lakshmi and to scare away the demons and the sister of Lakshmi, Alakshmi —the Goddess of Misfortune. This sister, however, was not born along with Lakshmi, but emerged with her from the Ocean of Milk when it was churned up by the gods.

It may be mentioned here that when the first born in a family is a girl, she is welcomed as Lakshmi—the Goddess of Fortune and Wealth. Lakshmi is called the Goddess of Beauty and Prosperity also.

Another reason given for illumination is that by Divali the sesamum crop (til) is ripe and is crushed; the new oil thus obtained is stored and the old oil is burnt in lamps to make the atmosphere within the house dry. The rainy season comes to an end just about twenty days before Divali and the houses are still damp. People light lamps to mark a season of crops also, especially rice and til, etc. Another idea given out is that all the insects that come into existence during the rainy season are attracted towards the lights and are burnt like moths and thus help the poor farmers by becoming manure for their fields!

DATTA JAYANTI

(Vindication of Anusiya)

ON the full-moon day of the month of Margashirsh falls the birthday of the god Datta. He was supposed to have been born at Akhalkop in Maharashtra where a temple built for him contains impressions of his footprints chiselled on slabs of stones. These footprints are worshipped on different occasions of the year, especially when fairs are held in his honour. There are one or two other places in the Western India where Datta has temples to his name, but ordinarily people worship him or observe his birthday at home. He is practically unknown in any other part of India.

The story of his birth throws some light on the human side of the gods. The three greatest gods, Shiva, Vishnu and Brahma, live up in the heavens together with their wives. Shiva is the Destroyer, while Vishnu is the Protector and Preserver of mankind and Brahma is the Creator. The name of Shiva's wife is Parvati, of Vishnu's wife Lakshmi, and Saraswati is the wife of Brahma. One day,

Vishnu happened to mention to his wife (or perhaps to all the three ladies) that Anusiya, the wife of the sage Atari, was the most virtuous woman on the face of the earth, and indeed, the best in the whole universe. When the ladies heard this, they felt jealous and began to think of a plan by which they might be able to belittle her in the eyes of their husbands as well as of the whole world, and might be able to convince their husbands that they three were the only women who remained unsurpassed in goodness and beauty of character. One day, the gods, after giving some time to the affairs of this world, and the ladies their househould affairs, sat down to play *Chauper* or *Chauser*, the wives on one side and the husbands on the other. The bet was that whichever party lost in the game would have to give a pledge to the winning party to carry out any behest which they might ask them to perform. As luck would have it, the ladies won, and the gods were all attention. The ladies asked the triad to go down to the earth and there do something to bring dishonour on the good Anusiya. The gods were sad when they heard it and knew not what to do. But they had to make good their promise, and therefore set out on their mission immediately. They disguised themselves as Sadhus or mendicants and approached Anusiya's door and begged for grains. Unfortunately her grains had been finished that very day, and she had therefore none in the house to give and her husband was away from home at that time. Being a true devotee, she felt ashamed that she could not give *bhiksha*, or alms to the Sadhus who had come in the name of God; as even now no beggar is turned away from a Hindu's house without receiving some alms. She prayed to Vishnu to have mercy on her and give her some grains to bestow on the Sadhus, not knowing that Vishnu himself was one of the mendicants. As she was a woman of great faith, Vishnu, who being a god, was everywhere, and had one 'self' in the heaven also, heard her prayers; and lo, her whole house was immediately full of grains. Piles upon piles of grain bags were found lying everywhere in the house. When she saw them, she thanked God and asked the Sadhus waiting outside to take away as much grain as they wanted. Thereupon the gods felt ashamed of what they had done to test her virtue at a time when she had no grains in her house to give them, and they returned to heaven more fully convinced of her virtue and goodness and faith and reported the matter to the ladies accordingly. When the three goddesses heard it, they were full of wrath, and they now took it upon themselves to bring dishonour and a bad name on Anusiya.

Without the knowledge of their husbands they slipped away from heaven quietly and came to the earth to do what they could to serve their end.

They alighted on the bank of a river which flowed in front of Anusiya's house, and there Lakshmi took the form of a very young girl, and Saraswati turned herself into a middle-aged woman, and Parvati became an old woman of eighty. The two women threw the young girl into the stream and raised a great hue and cry and shouted for help. The young girl, of course, could not be drowned; for being really a goddess, she was light and aerial in weight! However, when Anusiya heard the crying and wailing, she immediately ran to the scene, and without wasting a second, jumped into the water and saved the child. When the goddesses saw this, they were ashamed and rose up and went back to heaven crest-fallen!

But they were not appeased and wanted to try yet once more. This time they sent down their husbands again in the form of three Brahmins, dressed like Shankar Achariya, as great devotees of God. On hearing their voices, Anusiya came to the door and found herself face to face with the three Brahmin priests, and immediately bowed before them with clasped hands and waited for any order they might have to give. They demanded food to be served to them immediately as they were hungry. She was extremely happy to hear it as naturally she felt greatly honoured by their visit. But after hearing a happy assent from her they made one condition which was apparently quite impossible, and that was that she should prepare their food without her clothes on and serve it to them in the same manner, quite naked. She was very sorry to hear it but had to consent to it eventually as the Brahmins said that if she would not feed them they would die of hunger and the guilt of murder would be on her. Now no sin is so great as the killing of a Brahmin. One might kill so many other men and women and cows even, yet the sin would not be so hideous as the killing of one Brahmin! However, she trusted in God and prayed that He might save her from this ordeal.

It might be mentioned that their intention was to tackle her again as before in her hushband's absence who was away at the river for his bath. (A Hindu is supposed to take a bath three times a day; first, at the rising of the sun; secondly, at noon, and thirdly, at sunset, just when the sun is setting. He has to recite some *mantras* every time in worship of the sun, facing it and taking a little water in the joined palms of two hands, and letting it flow down. He can do this 'throwing of the water' as many times as he likes). So Anusiya's husband, before he left home, had done this ceremony at home, and then had gone to the river to take his bath. Ordinarily when this 'throwing of the water' is done at home, the water is generally dropped into the sacred Tulsi plant which every Hindu keeps in his house. If at the time of the oblations the plant is not near or is not in the house, this water can be collected in a flat copper basin in order to prevent the ground in the house from getting muddy. It was for this reason that Anusiya had collected the water of oblation in a flat basin which had been left unemptied by her husband.

To resume the thread of our narrative: when Anusiya found herself in this predicament, she suggested to the Brahmins to go to the river and take a bath as they usually do before taking food and in the meantime she would get their food cooked and ready to serve. After they departed, she stripped herself of her clothes and began cooking the food, and before they returned she had not only cooked everything but had 'laid the table' also, smearing the floor with a mixture of mud and cowdung and drawing different designs in chalk, and placing for them three big leaves in row from which to take their food. When everything was ready, she put on her clothes and awaited their arrival. It was in the forenoon that they arrived. She made them sit in their proper places, and they sat stripped of all clothes except the loin cloth—the common way in which Brahmins take their food. Now as the time of serving the food drew nigh she prayed to god Vishnu to protect her, and suggest to her the means whereby she might be able to circumvent their plot, and not be required to be naked in front of these grown-up men. As she prayed she took some water in her hand from the basin containing the oblation water left over by her husband, and sprinkled it in the name of the god Vishnu on the three men sitting in a row. No sooner had the water touched them than they turned into young infants. She took off her clothes now without feeling embarrassed, and as the infants could not take the food of grown up men, she put them on to her own breasts which were immediately filled with milk at the sight of the children.

The sage Narad keeps wandering about in the universe constantly, and is the messenger of gods and adviser of human beings. He is considered by some to be the son of the God Brahma also. Now when he found that the three great gods were in the house of Anusiya sucking her breasts in the form of babies he went up in haste, and informed their respective wives of the scandal. The wives immediately descended to the earth in great consternation. When they questioned Anusiya and demanded their husbands, she was greatly shocked to know what she had done, and fell on her face and craved their pardon saying that she was totally unaware of the fact that they were their husbands. However she suggested that as the children had sucked her breasts they should be left with her and to be brought up by her, she being childless. Of course, this was unacceptable to the goddesses and also to the gods! Anusiya then asked the goddesses to pick up their own husbands—a thing which they wanted to do immediately; but they were confused as the three children were alike in all respects and they could not say which was which. So they had to leave it to luck. When each one picked up a child it grew up into a full-sized man, and each lady found herself with another's husband; and as a result there was lot of confusion and blushing on the part of the goddesses! However when they resumed their original forms, they promised to let Anusiya have a child if she wanted one—a child which would be made of the combined Shakti or power of the three. On her agreeing with the proposal the three gods immediately made contribution of their respective Shaktis and they produced a child which was named Datta, signifying 'that which happens in the twinkling of the eye', something 'at once' and 'immediate'; and this because Datta was created by a quick and spontaneous action. This creation of Datta took place exactly at 12 o' clock noon. So the three were concentrated in one, and the result was the birth of a child having three faces, one trunk, four hands and two feet. He became on earth thus the incarnation of the three highest gods of heavens, who along with their wives were fully satisfied by the virtue of Anusiya, and her reputation as a virtuous woman remained for ever undisputed.

This child grew up in great wisdom, ability and learning, so much so that in course of time he became transformed into a god and is now worshipped as such. He was a great wanderer. In one day he would be in two or three different parts of India, taking his bath at one place, his food at another, and his rest at a third place, these stations being as far apart as Benares in the north and Kolhapur in southern Mahratta country. The name Dattareya—Datta, son of Atareya—is commonly used to express the wanderings of a man who is always on the move as 'Dattareya ki Pheri', which means (like) the wanderings of Dattareya. Nothing is known of his death; but the tradition is that he disappeared from this world at a place near the confluence of the rivers Panchganga and Krishna; and to perpetuate his memory a temple has been built at the exact spot of his disappearance. Fairs are held at this place for weeks at a time.

While in some places Dattareya is worshipped on the evening of his birthday, in other places the worship is done on other days. This worship is done by some on the seventh day before the full-moon day, or 9th, 5th, 3rd or one day before his birthday. Puja is done about six o'clock in the evening. He is worshipped as having within himself the essence of the three great Gods. The people hold meetings in which religious songs are sung and discourses given. These are called 'Kirtans' and 'Bhajans'. It does not matter so much if on the days before the actual birthday Kirtans, etc., are not held, but it is necessary that at exactly 12 o'clock of his birthday (the time at which Datta was born), there should be held Kirtans and religious sing-songs, and worship conducted. The rituals begin at 9 o'clock in the morning of that day, and are so timed that the whole thing is finished at 12 o'clock as in the case of the birth of Rama, the husband of Sita. As usual on such festivals, a fast is strictly observed.

THE END